ADVERSITY
BRINGS
BALANCE

ADVERSITY
BRINGS
BALANCE

FROM **OBSERVING**
YOUR LIFE TO
CREATING IT

AKÉ SATIA

Published by Advantage, Charleston, South Carolina.
Member of Advantage Media Group.

ADVANTAGE is a registered trademark, and the Advantage colophon is a trademark of Advantage Media Group, Inc.

Printed in the United States of America.

10 9 8 7 6 5 4 3 2 1

ISBN: 978-1-64225-318-4
LCCN: 2021925225

Cover design by Analisa Smith.
Layout design by Matthew Morse.

This publication is designed to provide accurate and authoritative information in regard to the subject matter covered. It is sold with the understanding that the publisher is not engaged in rendering legal, accounting, or other professional services. If legal advice or other expert assistance is required, the services of a competent professional person should be sought.

 Advantage Media Group is proud to be a part of the Tree Neutral® program. Tree Neutral offsets the number of trees consumed in the production and printing of this book by taking proactive steps such as planting trees in direct proportion to the number of trees used to print books. To learn more about Tree Neutral, please visit **www.treeneutral.com**.

Advantage Media Group is a publisher of business, self-improvement, and professional development books and online learning. We help entrepreneurs, business leaders, and professionals share their Stories, Passion, and Knowledge to help others Learn & Grow. Do you have a manuscript or book idea that you would like us to consider for publishing? Please visit **advantagefamily.com**.

To my wonderful Jessie. You are the best sister and friend one could ever hope for. I share this because I know that these are some of the lessons and words of encouragement you would pass on to me. You left so early, yet you gave more than one could ever ask for. Thank you for being the classic epitome of sacrificial love, kindness, grace, commitment, and perseverance. You are forever a beacon in my life and the reason why I dare to venture. I love you. Always. Forever.

CONTENTS

KNOW THYSELF

I am just the way I am.

Could this all be a dream? I wonder ...

How will I know when I have made it?

When my looks match my imagination?

When I'm ushered into worthy circles?

When my net worth reaches a certain level?

Questions yielding questions, answers not forthcoming

The answers seem reliant upon the approval of others

Perhaps living a life of falsehoods is the easiest way

Unbeknownst to me, it is a path of endless seeking

Where satisfaction is elusive, and contentment is evasive

Oh, no! This cannot be my story. There must be more.

I will find myself, meet myself, and know myself.

—AKÉ SATIA

Preface

Like many of us, I am motivated by two desires: to be personally fulfilled and to live in a world where others are also fulfilled. In my life journey, I noticed that every personal and professional accomplishment, though thrilling, left me with a fleeting sense of satisfaction and a lingering sense of longing. And by experiencing profound joy and living through agonizing experiences, I realized that my opportunity was to truly live—to explore, learn, grow, play, and share so that others may also benefit.

This realization led me down a path of self-discovery to understand who I am, why I am here, and what truly matters. My professional adventures and pursuits also strengthened my belief that organizations have a responsibility to propel individuals and society.

This story is anchored in the strength and belief that through life's challenges and despite our weaknesses, we can attain fulfillment. And I share this with vulnerability because the story is beyond me. Notably, this is not a panacea for life's challenges, so the idea is not to replicate what it entails. Instead, I hope you will become captivated by the idea of truly knowing yourself so that you can learn zealously, give intentionally, and grasp the opportunities that lie ahead of you.

Indeed, each of us is the heroine and the hero of our own story. And this is for anybody who aspires to thrive and to give all that they uniquely can. This story is for you and to you.

—Aké Satia
Maryland
October 6, 2021

Acknowledgments

Life is a journey of the heart, mind, and body. And I owe my existence and this endeavor to many remarkable women and men whose love and courage have propelled me. With humility, I thank them.

To my irreplaceable mom for always holding my hand, walking with me, and guiding me. To my selfless dad for setting a great example and giving unconditional support. To my sister, Jessie, for loving me wholeheartedly and inspiring me even when I cannot see her. To my sister, At, for being a second mom and best friend. To my brother-in-law, Darin, who started telling me several years ago that I had messages that needed to be shared. To my magnificent nephew, Nicholas, and effervescent niece, Hazel, for bringing immense joy.

To Aunty Mary N., who, when I was six years old, told me I was powerful. To Aunty Rose P., who constantly reminds me that God's footprints are my guide. To Aunty Mary M., who treats me like a daughter.

To cherished friends: Essi, for life-nourishing three-hour conversations; Marimargaret and Richard, whose lives are proof that your spirit can rejuvenate as you age; Leah, for reminding me of Jessie's impact; Pam, for allowing me to live vicariously through her as she enjoyed motherhood; and Rebecca and Meher, whose friendship transcended the workplace because it is seeded in the heart.

To Ms. Scotti and Ms. Solari, who taught me how to learn fervently. To Adana, Alicia, and Taryn, who showed me how to make an impact.

To great sources of inspiration: Simon Sinek, who publicly and through his book *Start with Why* inspired me by cogently sharing pearls of wisdom. To Brené Brown, whose book *The Gifts of Imperfection* planted a seed in my heart over ten years ago that changed my life.

And, most importantly, to my sole reason for being—my God, my One and Only.

Introduction

From cave drawings to hieroglyphics, from archaeological discoveries to historical biographies, from epics told orally and then scrolled on papyrus to viral videos posted for billions to instantaneously view on the internet, humanity has always defined itself through story. We consume fully fleshed out narratives that tell us what it means to be human. We eagerly piece together disparate elements of our collective experience to help us define what it means to be alive in this moment—and what it meant in moments past. This urge to narrativize is in our nature as a species and shows up as we lead our lives, trying to understand not only the world around us but our specific place in it—what we're here for and what we can offer. And just as every culture has its series of founding myths and legends—those intergenerational tales that define them and propel them forward—each of us has a life story that's authored with every breath. These life stories inform us of who we are and imbue our interpersonal interactions with personality and specificity.

In our collection of stories are a multitude of lessons, memories, and events that we return to and contemplate to find evidence of our defining characteristics—key attributes that make us who we are. On a good day, we turn to the positive moments to script our story: the moments when we were kind, or strong, or stood up for our values. On a bad day, however, that story changes. We focus on the ways in which we were weak, inadequate, made fun of, or embarrassed. Each of us has experienced both good and bad days—but why is it that the bad days are the ones that haunt us, as if it's *those* moments, or attributes, that represent who we *really* are? Why is it that when we are feeling down, all we can think of are the obstacles in our way—and not the many times we've overcome obstacles in triumph?

Creating My Story— and Helping You Create Yours

My own story is defined by the search for authentic fulfillment. Professionally, I help organizations grow and thrive by building a healthy workplace culture that empowers them to live their mission and cultivate a culture that is oriented on teamwork. I've driven business transformations for global organizations of varying sizes, enabling them to see and seize new opportunities to build a healthy culture, drive growth, and sustain relevance. I've led HR teams for the world's largest coffeehouse chain, orchestrating and directing initiatives to improve talent attraction and retention, catapult productivity, and accelerate innovation. At one of the world's leading tech corporations, I spearheaded growth for staff at various levels, drove leadership development initiatives, and enabled the reinvention of a comprehensive performance management approach for over fifty thousand staff members globally.

> To me, faith signifies the acknowledgment that I am not alone; that an Overarching Force and forces are accompanying me as I traverse my life journey and are propelling me along the right pathways.

Personally, I've built a meaningful life around my faith, relationships, and passions. While my career has shown there is power in numbers, my personal life has demonstrated that fulfillment can be found in authentic individual connections. To me, faith signifies the acknowledgment that I am not alone; that an Overarching Force and forces are accompanying me as I traverse my life journey and are propelling me along the right pathways. Along with my faith, I have fostered deep bonds with family and friends and sustained a years-long relationship as a sponsor to a special girl living in Lesotho.

As I grew into the person I am today, I experienced joy, but there were many moments in which the adversity I faced felt insurmountable. It's hard to not internalize the messages our culture gives us about who we are and how we are supposed to act. I didn't always like the way the world interpreted who I was based on what they saw on the outside, and I would be lying if I told you this interpretation didn't impact how I saw myself.

And yet, the events of my life, even the times when the obstacles before me felt too big to overcome, ultimately enabled me to discover my purpose, my passion, and my values. Through the highs and lows, I learned that I am who I am not in spite of my vulnerabilities but *because* of them. I learned that my strengths lie in my ability to embrace these vulnerabilities fully, without fear or shame.

> A person's intrinsic need to feel valued and to provide value informs many core decisions they make through the course of their lives.

My journey has led me to a place where I see transcending adversity as my secret superpower—and I'm passionate about helping others overcome the obstacles standing in their lives to grow, thrive, and shape the world into a better place.

Purpose of the Book

In this book, I want to share with you a little bit about the experiences that brought me here. But ultimately, this isn't about me and my journey—it's about you and yours.

As you'll see in the pages that follow, so much of the journey toward discovering our true essence involves overcoming adversity and realizing our unique strengths. I believe that helping people understand who they are—

what their story is—and what they can offer is one of the most impactful gifts a person can give. I also believe that a person's intrinsic need to feel valued and to provide value informs many core decisions they make through the course of their lives. It is my great hope that, in writing this book, I can help you make decisions that align with your deepest convictions and your truest self, using my life story as a backdrop. The goal is for you to be a creator, not an observer, of your life.

I also want to take a moment to note why I felt a particular urgency to write this book now—in this moment in history.

2020: The Ultimate Obstacle

In 2020, the COVID-19 pandemic threw a major obstacle at our planet that no one could escape. As best-selling author, optimist, and speaker Simon Sinek aptly said, "Crisis is the great revealer."[1] The pandemic forced each of us inside, not only physically into our home offices or makeshift workspaces but also mentally, into our deepest selves ... and what we found there didn't always sit well. With the world on pause, many of us had to stop living at breakneck speeds and take a good look at our lives for the first time in a long time, and existential questions naturally arose. Instead of asking *Who should I be?*, we started asking, *Who am I, really? Who are my true friends? Do I like my job? What are my deepest aspirations? Am I living up to my fullest potential? How can I balance all the roles I am called to play?*

As our personal and professional lives fused together, we had to reconsider how we navigate our lives, reconstruct our narratives, and ultimately reflect on why we do what we do. With work and life happening in the same place, we were also faced with conflicting priorities like never before. This was especially the case for women. In the modern workforce, women regularly have to battle all sorts of negative societal stereotypes about their value, talent,

---

1   Matt Haber, "Simon Sinek on How to Lead in a Crisis," *Inc.*, June 18, 2020, https://www.inc. com/matt-haber/simon-sinek-leadership-listening.html.

contribution, professional interests, ambition (or lack thereof), and so much more. As a result, women consistently find themselves in the challenging position of balancing work and life. The pandemic threw a wrench in that quest for balance. Suddenly, women had to make difficult decisions to step back from building their careers to help their children and families navigate ever-shifting changes, even if those same changes were wreaking havoc on their lives as well.

The pandemic also exposed a vacuum that already existed in society: the challenge we have in cultivating authentic relationships with intentionality. We became physically distanced and disconnected from one another.

The rise of technological advancements, specifically social media, has made it easier than ever to share opinions—and that is of great value. But social media has also replaced the hard work of true connection with a compulsion for endless likes and quick reactions. It takes a lot less time and effort to post a photo on Facebook or a tweet on Twitter and receive a hundred likes than to share the memory and context behind the photo or tweet with a friend. The pandemic offered a stark reminder of the chasm that exists between those two experiences—and what is lost when we don't reach out to connect.

The pandemic and the months that followed as the world reopened gave many of us ample time to observe—ourselves, our jobs, our connections, and so much more. Now, I want to help you move forward as an active participant in your own journey.

Overcoming Obstacles, One Chapter at a Time

This book is organized into five distinctive and interdependent parts, each with three interrelated chapters anchoring a unifying theme with the goal of helping you find what fulfills you, grounds you, and gives you meaning.

Part 1 is all about getting to know yourself and your mind. Within this section, I will talk about what it means to live authentically, and what steps you can take and specific reflections you can consider to make living authentically a hallmark of your story. I hope to give you the power to claim your identity, recognize what makes you special, and begin to make choices that help you live fully in both personal and professional spaces.

Part 2 is about self-development and growth. In this section, I will guide you to think about what personal growth looks like to you. I will also challenge you to get up close and personal with your flaws—or what you *think* your flaws are. In doing so, I will encourage you to exhibit self-love, to look at your whole self, to understand your tendencies and motives so that you can be strengthened and begin to embrace all of who you are.

Part 3 highlights the roles others play in our lives. Our journey to discovering ourselves and creating our lives requires major support! It's crucial that we maintain and prioritize connection with the people in our lives who truly see us and love us for who we are. It's equally crucial that we not give those who don't truly see us the power to create or shift our narratives. This section is all about cultivating that discernment and acting on it when needed.

Part 4 helps you start to make real decisions about your life. Being able to see situations clearly and act intentionally is a huge part of how we overcome the obstacles in our lives and create balance. The chapters in this section will help you gain the capacity and courage to decide what's right for you so that you know when to stay and when to walk away.

Part 5 represents the culmination of all you've learned. Now, you're ready to start creating your life the way you want. In this section, I will encourage you to dream about what your path could look like if fear were out of the picture. Fulfilling our dreams requires bravery and vulnerability. By the end of this section, it is my hope that you'll have plenty of both.

In each of these sections, I will share a bit of my story with you, including how I learned to manifest my superpowers from mistakes, how I made peace with my past, how I overcame the fears that prevented me from serving others, and how I learned to be deliberate and intentional in the decisions I make around my future. I want to share my story only inasmuch as it serves you to consider your own. As you read and reflect on these chapters, you might laugh, you might cry—but what you won't do is sit back and watch. While the chapters build off one another in a linear way, that doesn't mean your story has to follow suit. You might find you excel in some areas and struggle through others—and that's ok. It's your journey, and the struggle is part of how we grow and learn.

I hope you read this book with a sense of wonder. I also hope the pages within reawaken you to your lost dreams of making an impact. My ultimate hope for you is that as you finish those last pages, you embark on your journey purposefully and begin your search for fulfilment with a sense of realization and enchantment, anchored in a desire to embrace opportunity. Thank you for joining me—I'm so glad you're here.

PART 1

THE CALL TO ADVENTURE

CHAPTER 1

Know Thyself

Knowing oneself comes from attending with compassionate curiosity to what is happening within.

—GABOR MATÉ

Several years ago, I boarded a plane to China for a work trip and took my seat in business class. Shortly after, a flight attendant walked up to me and asked for my ticket. I handed it over to her and observed as she glanced at the ticket, nodded, and returned it to me. I also noticed that she didn't ask any of the other passengers—who all happened to be white men and women—for their tickets, including my colleague who was seated two rows ahead of me. So I gently asked the attendant, "Was there a problem?" She responded, "No, it's fine."

This flight attendant had clearly seen me and yet, in that moment, I was rendered completely invisible. She had decided to take what she perceived of me on the outside and make a stereotypical assumption of what I was capable of. It seemed my character was overridden by someone else's incorrect assumptions. I wondered if I should expose the issue, but as the moment passed, I decided to let it go. I needed to make that business trip, and I didn't want anything to stand in the way.

But I often wondered if my decision to "let it go" was the right decision.

Most people can think of a time when they felt undervalued, threatened, or stereotyped—a moment when they weren't seen for who they truly are. These moments, over time, can make us doubt ourselves. Exasperated by being singled out or made to "feel less than," we might succumb to the pressure to fit in and conform—to "just be like everyone else." But that thought raises an important question: While being like "everyone else" might make it easier to navigate life, does it lead to contentment and fulfillment?

As someone who grew up on three different continents, I've given a lot of thought over the years to what it means to "fit in." Moving around so often meant that the standard of acceptability often eluded me. Every few years, my peer group shifted along with schools, neighborhoods, languages, shopping trends, and everything in between. It didn't take me long to realize that conforming fully was never going to be an option for me. While this might sound like a liberating moment in my life, the real story isn't so simple.

Change can induce high levels of fear, even when the changes are positive. From a tender age, we learn that there is safety in conformity as we recall those moments when we didn't "dress the part," "say the right thing," or "make it on the right team." In those instances, we had to wrestle with the unknown and with fear because we didn't know what to expect. To avert fear, we "learned" it was essential to be like those around us: to conform. The problem is that conforming can be very limiting. Even worse, it can suppress creativity, discovery, playfulness, learning, and growth.

It can be difficult to reconcile what you think you know about yourself and what others say you are or must be in order to be accepted. Even if you release the burden of perfect conformity, preventing others' expectations and perceptions from getting to you and making you feel small or ashamed can be incredibly challenging.

As you live, who gets to tell your story? Whose expectations are dictating your choices: yours or someone else's? In this chapter, I want to address an important topic—in fact, it might be the single greatest question that each of us faces: Who are you *really*?

When I think about that business class flight to China, I remember being intent on not rocking the boat. If I faced the same situation today, I would speak up respectfully and clearly in the interest of myself and society. But today, my motivations are different than they were then.

So I look back on the woman I was then with a sense of compassion and an acknowledgment that I have grown, even though my response at the time left me uncertain for years if I'd said or done the right thing. When we know our values and ourselves, we are empowered and able to face challenges with integrity and own the outcome. And while we might be apprehensive about how our response was received, we can rest in the knowledge that we responded not from a place of fear but from a place of authenticity. And that is a beautiful thing.

> When we know our values and ourselves, we are empowered and able to face challenges with integrity and own the outcome.

The Heart-Work of Knowing Yourself

In my teenage years, I fostered a deep love of art and creativity, which has only grown since then. While I have plenty more to explore, I've been to enough art galleries and spent time with enough artists to know that the beauty and meaning of a work of art doesn't reside in how it is received. If the value of art were solely determined by the positive regard of others, we'd have a lot of boring, monotonous art in the world. But the goal of a true artist—a Michelangelo or a Vermeer—isn't approbation, but originality. Their work isn't a means to an end—the pure act of creation, of giving, is an end in itself.

Carl Jung said, "One does not become enlightened by imagining figures of light, but by making the darkness conscious."[2] As I mentioned earlier, the unknown is a scary place—and change can be even scarier. But when we begin to learn who we really are, what motivates us, what sparks joy in our lives, and where we add value, our lives become our blank canvas, and we are the master painter. Knowing ourselves is hard work, and it is heart-work, a vital and daring effort of getting in touch with your emotions, desires, and fears and facing whatever arises. What this can unleash is an awareness of your purpose and a desire to pursue what only you can uniquely give.

What can you uniquely give? When was the last time you felt free to dream, to be creative, and to play without judging yourself? As kids, dreaming is often a lot easier—knowing who you are and what you can offer can seem much more intuitive to grasp. As adults, we're often so conditioned by our environment to think and to show up in "acceptable" ways that dreaming and playing can seem elusive, perhaps childish. The key to seeing ourselves as we are often lies in remembering our childhood moments when we dreamt and played with abandon.

When I was in sixth grade, I befriended a girl named Fatima, who was shunned by the rest of the kids at school. Fatima was Muslim, and she came from a low-income family, while most of her peers were upper-middle-class kids with Catholic and Protestant backgrounds. Having a proclivity for marching to the beat of my own drum, I resisted joining a single group of friends. Instead, I chose to spend recess eating lunch with the "cool kids," then would break away and spend the rest of the time playing with Fatima.

After a while, I noticed that Fatima didn't always eat during recess. When I asked her why, she said she wasn't hungry. Fatima was very slim, so I figured she didn't like food that much. I later found out the real reason: her family couldn't afford to send her to school with lunch every day.

---

2   C. G. Jung and Hull Richard Francis Carrington, *The Philosophical Tree* (London: Routledge and K. Paul, 1967).

CHAPTER 1: KNOW THYSELF

I learned a lot from Fatima. I was curious about her hijab, which no one else at school wore, but which she wore with confidence. She often had henna tattoos, and one day she offered to do one for me. I was thrilled with the beautiful orange ink on my palm—it felt different, unique, and cool. Later, I started bringing snacks for Fatima so we could eat together at recess. I found that I enjoyed spending time with her just as much as I enjoyed the cool kids' company. So one day I suggested we all play together. The cool kids loved playing hopscotch, and Fatima, poised and tall, was particularly good at it, so they began wanting her to play on their team. Soon, my family had to relocate to a different country for my father's job. As I bade Fatima farewell, I left feeling I could've done more to help her fit in with the group.

When I reflect on my relationship with Fatima, it is emblematic of the person I am today. As a young child, I adamantly refused to view an individual's worth based on some arbitrary code. Helping friends like Fatima made me feel like a superhero, and the tendency to help the less fortunate is core to who I am. Ironically, I struggled to support myself in the same way. At the age of seven, I was regularly bullied by a classmate. I didn't tell anyone about it. Instead, I felt helpless. Even at that young age, I got down on myself and wondered why I didn't stand up for myself. I wondered, *Am I a superheroine or a coward?*

Do you remember the first time you felt deep shame as a child? In some ways, it feels like a fall from innocence. You spend your early childhood feeling like you're perfect just as you are. But as soon as someone tells you differently, you struggle to get rid of the image they painted of you from your mind.

"Am I Doing This Right?"

At some point in childhood, many of us relinquish the power over our own narrative to others. We let our peers decide who we are, what we should be, and how we should act. Suddenly, instead of thinking about what we want to do, we are driven to find out what we "should" do. Instead of opening up to our shame and our vulnerabilities, we're often inclined to hide them and build up a protective fortress around them so that nobody else can see them.

If fitting in and social approval were the ticket to contentment, once we are good enough at answering the "should" questions and the door of acceptance opens to us, we should feel endless bliss. But instead, when the door of social approval is opened to us, more often than not all we feel is fear that it could be shut at a moment's notice. The truth is letting others define us "saves" us from the hard work of defining ourselves. But if there's one thing more exhausting than trying to live up to others' expectations, it's the fatigue that stems from trying to suppress and ignore our real selves, including our needs, desires, and fears.

Based on my personal and professional experiences, I have a hunch that *everyone*—even the assumingly most powerful and those we think have it all figured out—still hear a little voice inside their head asking, "Am I doing this right?" and "Am I enough?" What I have learned is that people who truly know themselves don't muzzle that tender voice in fear of what it might reveal. Instead, they listen to it, and they let it teach them. They know that striving toward authenticity and aiming to embrace every part of one's self is foundational to living a fulfilled life.

The Value of Knowing Yourself

After my childhood bullying experience, I worked hard to define myself against what I saw as a fundamental weakness: my inability to stand up for myself. I sought adventure and knowledge, hoping that life experience would cement my "superhero" status. I went years thinking I was either one or the other—a coward or a heroine—because I certainly couldn't be both. After all, there's no such thing as a "cowardly Wonder Woman." Over the course of my own journey of getting to know myself, I finally realized that it is only by accepting both of these seemingly opposed sides that I can truly know and love myself as a whole person—flaws and all.

Some people misunderstand deep personal exploration to be an act of selfishness, or even narcissism. In reality, it is the opposite. It is only once we find deep acceptance for ourselves that we can begin to truly offer our gifts to others with ease. The reason is deceptively simple: when we don't accept ourselves, we often do things as a means to an end. We don't help others because we want to but because we feel obliged to do so by those pesky "shoulds." But when we act in a way that aligns with who we really are, our actions—like the great artists—become an end in themselves. We no longer give because we should—we give because we derive deep meaning from it. We are the painters of our life's canvas, and we choose our mediums and colors because we like their effects.

I once knew an elderly gentleman who was deeply knowledgeable about gardening and had the most beautiful grass lawn in the neighborhood. Everyone admired his lawn and requested his advice. Soon, rather than just advising, he started taking care of his neighbors' lawns. Suddenly, he was tending to over twelve lawns! What was once a gift had become a burden to him. He felt an obligation to meet his neighbors' expectations—and yet he was receiving no joy from the experience. After wrestling with the fear of no longer being seen as the cherished neighbor, he conferred with some friends. Then, he informed his neighbors that he will continue to give them advice on how to keep their lawns in exquisite shape but could no longer take care of the lawns himself. Appreciative of his help over the years and his honesty, neighbors stopped asking him to work on their lawns but continued to solicit his input and encouraged new neighbors to do the same. He continued to be seen as an esteemed neighbor and was able to serve freely.

Reflect and Imagine ...

Knowing oneself authentically requires confidence. It enables us to exit the passenger seat and assume the driver's role in our life journey, taking ownership of our choices, decisions, and the ensuing outcomes. With that in mind, take a moment to reflect on the following:

We all have strengths and weaknesses. But sometimes, it can be easy to think of ourselves as a collection of shortcomings, and exposing that collection to people who could reject us is terrifying. However, it's important for us to know that we are fully seen and truly known by others.

> Knowing oneself authentically requires confidence. It enables us to exit the passenger seat and assume the driver's role in our life journey, taking ownership of our choices, decisions, and the ensuing outcomes.

Simon Sinek gives a simple tip to embark on the path of being vulnerable: start small.[3] Exposing our greatest fears, weaknesses, or needs with a group of strangers as a first step might not be prudent. Instead, it's helpful to start with a trusted friend. Taking a leap of faith that they'll be able to hold our "secret" without judgment helps us feel confident that it's ok to expose more of ourselves.

---

3   Simon Sinek, "How to Start in Being More Vulnerable," YouTube, February 4, 2021, https://www.youtube.com/watch?v=_lDl0ri32h0.

Think of a friend that you trust enough to share a weakness or struggle with. What do you need from them? Are you asking for help or encouragement or just hoping to "get things off your chest"? Knowing this will help you decide how to share and what to ask for.

• • •

As we conclude this chapter, I want to emphasize that no other person— including your coworkers, your acquaintances, or society at large—should create your story. So ask yourself again: "Who is creating my story?"

When we submit to the pressure to conform or fit in, we tailor out those qualities that we deem unfit or plain weird. But what if I told you those qualities could reveal your superpowers?

CHAPTER 2

Your Uniqueness Is
Your Superpower

I thought not fitting in was something I had to
fix. Now I see it as my superpower.

—MAXIME LAGACÉ

Movies and television transport us to worlds where anything is possible. When we're young, most of us wonder what it would be like to have special abilities—to fly at maximum speed like Supergirl, to have super strength like Wonder Woman, or some combination of both. As a kid, I remember watching *Wonder Woman* and feeling certain that if I focused hard enough, I could fly from my bedroom to my best friend's house in the blink of an eye and return in time for dinner. I also remember the feeling of sore disappointment when I noticed that I was still in my bedroom, despite how hard I clenched my fists and willed it.

When I finally realized that no amount of concentration would help throttle me into the air with grace and ease, I had to admit I was a mere mortal among other mortals. And that meant admitting something even worse: I was just another average kid.

No kid—or adult, for that matter!—wants to be average. And yet, as I discussed in chapter 1, no kid wants to be all that different either. Once our "superhero" dreams fade, we seek out more easily recognizable talents to set ourselves apart. But what if, in our search for the right balance between fitting in and standing out, we miss out on learning the things that truly set us apart?

While we humans may yet lack the ability to fly, each of us has capabilities and tendencies that make us uniquely special and able to undertake specific activities. At its most basic, a superpower is something of value that we are uniquely positioned to offer. This would include the specific inclinations and abilities that each of us can leverage to provide value through the course of our lives. In this chapter, I want to help you begin to explore what those tendencies and capabilities are and how they can help you contribute to making the world a better place.

What Is a Real Superpower ... and How Can I Find Mine?

When we watch our favorite fictional superheroes on screen or read about them in comics, we marvel at the sheer invulnerability of their talents and the utter effortlessness by which those talents are displayed. Wonder Woman's flying moves came so easily to her that, when they didn't for me, it didn't take me long to shrug my shoulders in defeat. *Something must be wrong with me. I'm not naturally good at this, so it must not be my thing. I'm not that special*, I thought.

> A superpower is something of value that we are uniquely positioned to offer.

As adults, we can all sympathize with how easy it is for a kid to jump to this conclusion. And we all know on a gut level that this conclusion is wrong. But how many of us can explain why?

The answer may be found in the parts of those superhero sagas that tend to get less focus: the origin stories. Many of our classic heroes didn't begin as gods but as ordinary men and women who stumbled into their powers through a trick of fate, followed by significant struggle. In these origin stories, impenetrable strength and stately valor are replaced by vulnerability, doubt, and confusion. Our soon-to-be heroines and heroes had no idea their mishaps would shape them as they would. I believe there are lessons to be found in their journeys toward greatness that apply to our own.

> Our superpowers are often revealed to us when we know what we love, why we stand out, how we offer value to others, and where we derive fulfillment.

Imagine if Peter Parker looked at the gossamer spinning out of his wrists and thought to himself, *I'd better start wearing long sleeved T-shirts to cover this up.* Imagine if every time his Spidey sense flared up, instead of paying attention to it, he used the moment to lament his inability to fully read minds, like other superheroes!

Now, imagine another scenario. Wonder Woman's origin story involves being molded from clay on an all-female island and granted superhuman gifts by the Greek gods themselves. But one day, she must leave the island, and all she knew, behind. Facing uncertainty in a new land, she had a decision to make: she could either work to overcome the challenge of applying her superhuman skills to this foreign place, or she could decide such a challenge was just too complicated. The fact that she chose the former instead of the latter is what makes her a superhero. If she had given up, well, that wouldn't have made for much of a story.

Take your own favorite superhero and imagine what their story would look like if they decided to use their powers for other, less heroic reasons. The difference between a hero and a villain isn't the superpower itself but how that power gets used—the hero uses their powers for good while the villain uses their powers for evil. Along those lines, if our heroes used their gifts solely for their own benefit, they wouldn't be heroes *or* villains; they'd just be selfish.

As stated earlier, we humans all have unique capabilities and tendencies, but instead of focusing on what we can give, we often focus on what we lack. We can spend our whole lives lusting after someone else's superpowers— another person's innate charisma, or their quick wit. And in doing so, we miss out on our own gifts hiding in plain sight. Our superpowers are often revealed to us when we know what we love, why we stand out, how we offer value to others, and where we derive fulfillment.

Maybe you can't remember the last time you wondered what it would be like to fly. But can you remember the last time you reflected on what makes you uniquely and wonderfully *you*? Maybe you can't read minds, but perhaps your insightfulness enables you to offer invaluable advice. Maybe you can't teleport, but you have a gift of empathy that helps others feel seen. The superhero stories I shared may seem silly on the surface, but when you dig a little deeper, they give context and specificity to what a superpower *really* is. Super speed is useless if its owner has never tried to run fast, and certainly means nothing if it doesn't help people in some greater way.

I suggested a few paragraphs earlier that a superpower is something that you are uniquely positioned to offer the world. As you consider various life situations and experiences where you've given back in some way—to a person, team, or community—what patterns begin to emerge about your behavior? Are you willing to "flex" whatever skill you've brought to the table so that it grows stronger over time? Most importantly, when you think about developing those skills, can you see how doing so could make a positive impact on people's lives? Because that's what superpowers are really all about: they are our unique tools that, when developed, enable us to serve others and leave us with a sense of fulfillment.

How Your Superpower Can Change the World

Has a friend or a coworker ever said to you, "I think you'd be really good at this!" If they have, what was your response? I've had plenty of these moments where, upon hearing that feedback, I shrugged it off, assuming I probably didn't have what it takes. What if, in those moments, we instead asked ourselves, "What are they seeing in me that I am not seeing in myself?" We tend to think a superpower is something that mysteriously benefits us without exactly knowing how or why. This vagueness can make it difficult to effectively apply our unique capabilities in real-world settings. In this section, I want to show you how you can start getting intentional about your superpowers to make a tangible impact.

Being Different Cultivates Empathy

Over the course of my life, I've had to assimilate into different cultures, speak different languages, and navigate the business world as both a woman and a minority. One of the greatest lessons I've learned is that when you are different, the majority won't change to make you comfortable. When we encounter differences—whether in people, situations, or experiences—we can become apprehensive or even fearful. While this may initially evoke a desire to conform, what is most beneficial in these moments is to instead maintain a sense of curiosity and openness so that we can observe with a nonjudgmental mindset and learn.

In order to thrive, it's important to approach every interaction in a manner that doesn't diminish who we are and doesn't diminish others.

I would like to emphasize that the more we strive to conform, the more we lose track of the things that make us special. In order to thrive, it's important to approach every interaction in a manner that doesn't diminish who we are and doesn't diminish others. By staying true to ourselves, yet meeting every moment with curiosity and openness, we can see situations through another person's lens without simply ceding to their view.

Difficulty Builds Perseverance—and a Purpose

In my professional work, I help people and organizations realize what they can offer and how they can thrive. This often entails guiding organizations to refine their strategy, set their direction, and communicate effectively to gain support, mobilize their plan, and execute it successfully. One of the companies I worked with was a real estate marketing company that had undergone a merger and multiple executive-level changes. After two years, the company was still struggling to define and articulate a clear strategy. During this period of uncertainty, there was low productivity, low employee morale, and lingering fear of an impending acquisition. Based on my professional experiences, I knew that while no single prescribed approach would change this culture, a collaborative and inquisitive approach would likely yield a desired outcome. This required listening, brainstorming, inspiring, enabling, and taking action.

In addressing this challenge, I faced two major hurdles. First, low morale and fear-based thinking created an environment of mistrust in the organization. People were afraid to be candid, and even more afraid to be vulnerable. Second, I didn't speak the real estate "language." Every business arena has its own vocabulary and insider knowledge. As a consultant, I'm accustomed to entering spaces as an outsider. In this case, my innate curiosity and insight enabled me to learn and, in partnership with the team, uncover the appropriate approach to help the company regain its footing.

Figuring out what we do well is often born out of struggle and persistence. And great insights often emerge during our most trying times. That was certainly the case for me in this situation. Being purposeful and persevering are some of the key ingredients for overcoming challenging situations.

Constant Change Helps You Learn

The world is ever changing, and the 2020 pandemic reinforced this point. When we reflect on Wonder Woman's story, we recall that she dared to move to a foreign land and recognized that hard work and intention were required for her to successfully apply her superpowers. The same applies to us. In many instances, situations arise in which we are called to adapt, and this can constitute the most fertile ground for learning as we discover what is unique about us and where we struggle. As Oprah Winfrey said, "The greatest discovery of all time is that a person can change his future by merely changing his attitude."

The more we look at moments of change not as insurmountable obstacles but as opportunities to grow, the more in touch we'll become with our superpowers and what we can offer to the world.

Reflect and Imagine ...

Everyone has a superpower—and if you're willing to learn what it is, how to flex it, and how to use it, you'll be your own kind of unstoppable. Here's a way to identify opportunities.

Cultivate your ability to spot an assumption. Our assumptions about the grandness of the world and our relatively small place in it can prevent us from seeing what makes us unique and limit our ability to apply our capabilities. If we want to embrace our superpowers, we need to get curious. With this in mind, consider the following:

Remember a time when you've said, "I always x, y, or z," or "I never x, y, or z." Where do those thoughts come from? If these thoughts weren't true, what could be possible? What would you do differently?

Next time you're frustrated with someone you don't get along with, ask yourself: Does this person intend to hurt me? Why do I think so? What benefits does this person offer? What's one thing I could do to connect with them? A balanced view of others allows us to see opportunities in challenges.

• • •

We might be inclined to think of ourselves as either a superhero or a coward. The reality is at times we display extreme acts of courage, and at other times we shrink back. You gain power when you realize that, at your core, both qualities of courage and fear reside in you. You have the ability to be brave or to cower in fear, and it is always a choice.

CHAPTER 3

It Starts with a Choice

*What you decide not to do is probably more
important than what you decide to do.*

—DANIEL PINK

In writing this book, I understand the gift I can give is primarily motivational: by sharing my journey through adversity, I hope to help you navigate your own challenges and ultimately find balance. I also understand that there is a limit to what these words can do. You see, all I can do is present you with my insights. It is up to you to decide what to do with them. Knowing yourself and what makes you unique enables you to understand what you can give and what you are *capable* of giving the world.

You can know yourself inside and out. You can spend a whole lifetime reflecting and honing your unique skill set. But unless you make a conscious choice to apply that knowledge accordingly, your reflections can only go so far. The prior chapters in part 1 were all about how we view things. In this chapter, it's time to explore how we *do* things. How do we make a choice? And why is the act of choosing so important?

The Choice I Made

Over the years, I was driven by a desire for self-knowledge. I wanted to know who I was and why I was here. I made a commitment to myself: when the time arrives to do something new, or when a current environment no longer serves me, I would make a change. Each time I made a major change, I reminded myself that although I might be scared, the alternative—being stagnant—would be far worse. I could stay put and exist in a state of complacency, or I could take a risk and thrive. As I learned what I was good at, I felt the world needed more from me than mere subsistence. It needed the gifts that only I could uniquely contribute.

Then, in my early thirties, being an avid walker and lover of adventures like skydiving and ballroom dancing, I received news I wasn't ready for: a diagnosis of multiple sclerosis (MS).[4] This was a serious test to the commitment I'd made to myself to experience life with a zest for learning. Could I really put the commitment into action?

Before this point in my life, I'd faced plenty of challenges. But my MS diagnosis was a greater challenge still. MS has neither a predictable timeline nor a known cure—yet. Sometimes people lose their ability to walk before they're diagnosed or after. In other cases, people continue walking and can participate in their normal activities for the rest of their lives. I had very limited knowledge of the condition when the doctor first shared the news. What I did understand was his suggestion that, sometime in the future, I might benefit from a walking aid. Suddenly, I had to reckon with the possibility of being constrained to what I viewed as a lifestyle of limited adventure and growth. The news was devastating.

---

4   I was fortunate my doctor diagnosed me when he did, but if I had known what I do now, that diagnosis may have come a lot earlier. If you are experiencing symptoms you can't easily explain, don't be afraid to ask your doctor for help. Early detection can improve MS outcomes. For more resources, check out the back pages of this book.

A few years after the MS diagnosis, I moved back to Maryland to be closer to family. I was already struggling to walk, and the realization that I might soon need assistance terrified me. In my twenties and early thirties, I would regularly go on long walks with friends. Now, I was hesitant to walk around my neighborhood. I was afraid to fall, but I was even more afraid of what people would think of me if they saw me tripping on sidewalks.

Still struggling to make a choice about how I was going to proceed in the face of my adversity, I decided to resume my walking habit at dawn, when fewer people could see me and my perceived weakness. I needed support on my walks from someone who could accompany me without judgment—no placating and no pity, just support. My mother was that person, and I couldn't have asked for a better partner on my journey.

When she was in her early seventies, my mom was hit by a car on a crosswalk. The incident fractured both of her ankles. If I were her, in that moment I would've thought I'd reached the end of my walking days. Yet she made it to the other side of a grueling recovery process and was back on her feet for brisk hour-long walks within a few months. The deep sense of resolve and optimism she displayed in meeting her own adversity inspired me. When I observed her life, I saw someone who never shut the door in her own face— and as we walked together, I started wondering how I could do the same.

Prior to being diagnosed with MS, I saw my body as a system I could master. Making the choice to work with my diagnosis instead of fighting against it would require a new kind of mastery. After a few weeks of walking at dawn, I could feel my balance improving, and with my mother's encouragement, I grew confident enough to start walking during regular daylight hours and to start building habits that would help me master my new lifestyle.

This story represents one moment of intentional choosing that served to guide my path forward. Can you think of a time in your life when you were called to make a choice? As you deliberated, what factors guided your ultimate decision? Carlos Castaneda once wrote, "The basic difference between an

> You can either observe your life floating by, or you can choose to be at its helm—but make no mistake, you *always* have a choice.

ordinary man and a warrior is that a warrior takes everything as a challenge, while an ordinary man takes everything as a blessing or a curse."[5] You can either observe your life floating by, or you can choose to be at its helm—but make no mistake, you *always* have a choice. So what will you choose—and how will you decide?

Overcoming Fears and Fantasies

As you grow and evolve, you inevitably face new situations that require intentional decision-making. Examining what's motivating you is a key component of making a deliberate choice about your future. Motivation can take many forms. However, there are two factors that can cloud your vision of what's possible. Fear and fantasy are two sides of the same coin—a coin that happens to be a particularly dangerous one to trade in when making a choice.

The Problem with Fear

If you've ever embarked on a risky physical challenge—like kite surfing or skydiving—then you know that some decisions can induce high levels of fear, even when the impacts of those decisions are likely to be positive. When faced with the opportunity to make a change that will lead you to a better place, you might be tempted to hang on to the past out of fear. But fear is not a good reason to stay put. In our journey toward making intentional choices about how we lead our lives, fear is an enemy we must move past in order to move forward.

---

5   Carlos Castaneda, *Tales of Power* (New York: Pocket Books, 1992).

In chapter 1, we took an in-depth look at conformity—and why, if we want to figure out who we really are, we should steer away from mindless conformity. When it comes to making choices in our lives, the pressure to conform can be a difficult motivator to uproot often due to fear. You see, we tend to gravitate toward conformity when we are fearful of what might happen if we choose to go down our own path. Conforming to the crowd allows us to move about the world within clear boundaries of what's acceptable, and our ability to "fit in" shields us from the dangers of getting too close to the boundary lines.

But as much as the boundary lines seem to protect you, they also hem you in and limit your potential. And there comes a time in life when you must decide whether staying shielded is more important than offering your gifts to the world. The pressures of conforming would have you believe that pursuing anything outside of those neatly drawn lines will not end well. But the truth is that those lines are arbitrarily drawn—and nobody can really predict what will happen when you cross them and move into uncharted territory. If that seems terrifying, that's to be expected. Just remember, the biggest thing that separates the summit from the base of the mountain is the choice to make the climb.

Fear will always show up in your journey, but you can learn to recognize the good, motivating fear from the limiting kind by watching how it appears in your mind. When I was deciding whether and under what conditions I would start walking again in Maryland, a lot of my considerations included the word "should": "I shouldn't walk during daylight hours because if I fall, others will belittle me." Perhaps you've used this word in making your own decisions. So let me ask you: Who's telling you what you should or shouldn't do?

Upon reflection, I realized my own "should" statements were motivated by one key question: "Am I enough?" Other questions—like "*Will I be accepted?*"—soon followed. It seems to me that whoever gets to decide the answers to those questions is the same person telling us we "should" do this or that ... and in most cases, that person isn't *you*.

When you are motivated by fear, and by "shoulds," you give others the power to determine your next steps, and in essence determine your future. Living authentically means putting ourselves in the position of "I choose" as much as possible. The greater the choice in front of us, the greater the fear we are likely to face. And yet, once you reach your summit, you'll thank yourself for choosing to trust the path that brought you there, and that's a pretty empowering reward.

The Problem with Fantasy

While fear might be the biggest enemy when it comes to making a choice, its flip side—fantasy—is just as dangerous. In making decisions, we often ignore the things we can control while placing too much value on the things we can't. When the things we can't control become our primary motivation, we relinquish our power. For example, if you take on a project at work with the sole aim of impressing your boss and getting a promotion, your efforts might feel futile if you are not promoted. Salary increases, recognition, and other desires are never guaranteed, and when our satisfaction is entirely dependent upon the goodwill or actions of others—something we have no control over—we are setting ourselves up for disappointment, no matter how strongly we believe we deserve what we seek.

When our satisfaction is entirely dependent upon the goodwill or actions of others—something we have no control over—we are setting ourselves up for disappointment, no matter how strongly we believe we deserve what we seek.

When we fantasize about achieving a certain outcome, we focus less on the journey and solely on the destination. And the frustration of achieving anything less than that outcome also makes quitting seem a lot easier than persevering through another disappointment. In either case, we run the risk of robbing ourselves of the joy and value the journey can provide. Once we can overcome the dual temptations of letting our fears or our fantasies decide our life path for us, we can start moving forward with intention and choosing wisely.

Choosing Intentionally

At face value, making a choice that is aligned with who we are can seem a lot harder than the alternative, but it's a whole lot easier in the long run. Deciding with an "I choose" versus an "I should" mindset provides ownership over your ultimate decision. If you get the desired outcome, you can trace your success back to the deliberate choices that helped you get there. And if things don't pan out as desired, you have the opportunity to reflect and learn. In contrast, when you decide based on fear or fantasy and things go well, it feels serendipitous or lucky—and because the focus was more on the outcome than the process, you may not know how to replicate your success. Also, if things don't go well, the lack of accountability for your decision may lead you to blame others instead of reflecting on what you could've done differently, thereby increasing the likelihood of making the same mistake again.

We make wiser choices when we respond rather than simply react to our circumstances. And sometimes the best response is *deciding to wait*. Life entails navigating peaks and valleys—high points and low points. But most often, we find ourselves in the plains, which can feel a little mundane at times. However, that doesn't mean they're not just as important to your growth. It took me a while to come to my decision to face MS instead of blaming the disease for co-opting my life plans, and I faced plenty of days where I was simply treading water. But during that period, I learned that how we wait is just as important as the waiting itself. When a flower seed is planted in the ground, the time that passes before something bursts through the soil is not wasted. The seed is getting the nourishment it needs to thrive and survive when it finally emerges. Taking the time to observe, consider, and collect the relevant facts before making a big decision can make our resolve even stronger.

Reflect and Imagine ...

Think about an important decision you made recently: **Who—or what—influenced your decision?** Paying attention to when you say you "should" do this or that is one great way to tell whether fears, desires, or others are determining your choices.

Another great question to ask yourself is: **What have I always wanted to do that I haven't pursued?** Perhaps a skill or a relationship you'd like to build. What holds you back from doing it? Fear? Time? Others' expectations? What's one thing you could do to move forward?

• • •

As I stated at the beginning of this book, this story is not about me and my journey—it's about you and yours. As you've read through part 1, I hope you've begun to envision yourself as an active participant in creating your own story, rather than a spectator. Notably, at some point, you'll face a pivotal decision: Will you proceed on your journey of exploration with the desire to give all you can, or will you stay where you are? Whenever you are ready to make that choice, part 2 will help you put your courage to good use. I look forward to continuing on this journey with you!

PART 2

BEGIN YOUR JOURNEY

CHAPTER 4

Relentlessly Pursue Growth

We can't become what we need to be by remaining what we are.

—OPRAH WINFREY

As you've reflected on your life, you realize there's more to you, and the realm of possibility to grow, explore, and thrive is greater than you can imagine. You also know that you can offer more, and you've made the courageous choice to see what awaits you on the path less followed—the path that leads you toward your authentic self. So what now? Now that you've answered the call, how do you begin this journey?

Being open to learning, changing, and self-exploration is in some ways the greatest choice you'll make on this path. As living beings, we are always changing. And we are afforded opportunities to progress, regress, or stagnate. In our pursuit of our authentic selves, the key is to change in the right direction ... in other words, to grow. Merriam-Webster defines growth as progressive development; evolution; an increase or expansion.[6] To me,

---

6   "Growth," definition and meaning, Merriam-Webster, accessed November 19, 2021, https://www.merriam-webster.com/dictionary/growth.

personal growth is the product of intentional positive choices you make over time and amid all sorts of life events, big and small, that eventually lead to a lifetime of blossoming.

As you reflect on your life now, in what direction are you headed and what are you growing toward? Are you happy about that direction? Part 2 is all about beginning your journey with intentionality. Getting what we desire or need often requires growth. In this chapter, I want to give you the tools to grow in the direction that gives you purpose and makes you hungry for the pursuit itself.

What Does It Take to Grow?

When I was a child, I dreamed of becoming a pianist. People often told me my long fingers were "meant for the piano." Taking those comments to heart, I asked my parents to sign me up for lessons, watched videos of pianists I admired, enrolled in music theory classes, and imagined the day my long fingers would gracefully stroke the piano keys on stage, rousing multiple standing ovations around the world.

To this day, people still comment that my fingers must make me a great pianist. It might disappoint them to learn that, in fact, I can't even play a D-flat major chord on a keyboard anymore. So what happened?

I nursed the idea that I could be a great pianist until I was in my late twenties—but "could" is the operative word. While I might have had the potential, I was never fully committed. I never had the relentless determination to give up comforts like forgoing playdates with my friends after school for piano lessons, and I never had the long-game intentionality to really build the skill set that would've brought my potential to fruition.

We all have our own list of "coulds"—those things we just have a hunch we'd be great at if we ever decided to give it a shot. And it sure seems easier to simply trust that hunch than to test it out. After all, what if we fail? In several cases, making the choice not to pursue your "coulds" is relatively inconsequential. But sometimes, these forgone opportunities cost us more than we'd like to admit. What would've happened if Einstein just assumed he *could* be a genius, rather than actually trying to solve the world's problems? What if Beyoncé told herself she *could* be one of the greatest performers of our time but decided she'd rather just sit on the couch instead?

So many of us inadvertently treat our potential like a treasure that, when found, we mustn't spend. But keeping our potential out of sight, under lock and key, is a lose-lose situation. On one hand, what lies behind that protected door could be inconsequential. On the other hand, behind the door could reside a treasure with the power to change the world—but what good is it to anyone when it's all locked up? Growth is a process of creation, and creation is a vulnerable pursuit—one that's a necessary first step on our journey toward finding and knowing our true selves. If you're willing to find out what potential gems you might be sitting on, I have four keys to help you unlock the door.

> Personal growth is the product of intentional positive choices you make over time and amid all sorts of life events, big and small, that eventually lead to a lifetime of blossoming.

First, Be Committed

Sources have suggested that the average person makes thirty-five thousand decisions every day.[7] If you sleep for seven hours a day, that breaks down to about two thousand decisions every hour you're awake! But as we all know, all decisions are not weighted equally, so obsessively worrying over every decision we make can leave us so overwhelmed that nothing of significance ever gets

---

7 Eva M. Krockow, "How Many Decisions Do We Make Each Day?" *Psychology Today*, September 27, 2018, https://www.psychologytoday.com/us/blog/stretching-theory/201809/how-many-decisions-do-we-make-each-day.

accomplished. This state of mind is not beneficial for setting and sticking to goals. In such a state, even your own well-being can become just another obligation.

That's why commitment is the first and most foundational step toward pursuing growth. Making a positive choice once is admirable. But committing to make that choice over and over again is what brings about long-lasting change.

If you're worried your power to commit might get subdued by being overwhelmed or decision fatigue, there's a simple solution: make your choice to commit steadfast, unaffected by circumstance or trials. Former Harvard Business School professor Clayton Christensen notes, "It's easier to hold your principles 100 percent of the time than it is to hold them 98 percent of the time."[8] The reason for this is simple—when you're not all in, you give yourself permission to doubt, to make excuses, and to give up.

Because I wasn't 100 percent committed to my piano lessons, I had to constantly ask myself if I'd rather hang out with my friends or practice piano. At a tender age, unaware of the long-term benefits of becoming masterful at the piano, practicing never sounded like the more appealing option. Not eating the dessert will rarely sound more appealing than indulging in the decadence. What are some examples in your own life where 98 percent commitment isn't quite cutting it? How might your life change if you committed that extra 2 percent?

Next, Be Curious

Once you've committed to growth, you might begin to wonder how you can put this notable commitment into action. The next step to unlocking your potential is to get curious about all the ways you might grow. One great place

---

8   Benjamin Hardy, "The 100 Percent Rule That Makes Life a Lot Easier," *Psychology Today*, April 24, 2020, https://www.psychologytoday.com/us/blog/quantum-leaps/202004/the-100-percent-rule-makes-life-lot-easier.

to start is to take a moment to reflect and remember. What have you done well at various stages in life? What moments in your life are you most proud of—and what do they reveal about the potential unique skills and abilities you have and can nourish?

When looking back on our lives, many of us too often focus on the missed opportunities, the roads not taken, and the regrets. Don't let the present moment of reflection turn into another missed opportunity for growth in your life. Our pasts hold gems and sores alike—and both offer us lessons on how we might evolve.

In chapter 2, we discussed how reflecting on what you enjoy giving to others and what you're good at can lead you to discover what you can uniquely offer. By getting curious, these reflections can also lead you to uncover behavioral patterns in your life that sustained your abilities before you even knew what they were. Sometimes, we are so compelled to act that our action doesn't feel like a choice. Maybe when you see a friend in need of a hug or comforting, you simply meet the moment without a second thought—or maybe, during a business brainstorm meeting, you never shy away from breaking the ice first. Getting curious about our past can help us connect the dots and find patterns that can lead us toward more intentional growth in the future.

Many of us are wired to want a road map before we set off on a journey. By reflecting and being open to what we find, we can start to build the map for ourselves—one that is tailor-made to our unique pursuits.

Third, Be Intentional

Intentionality is key to growth. Spotting trends in our behavior and recognizing the patterns in our experiences helps us grow. In time, I realized that the experience I described in chapter 1 of being discriminated against on a plane was closely tied to my experience of being bullied as a kid. The key difference was the level of sophistication. As a kid, I had a backpack, storybook, and colored pencils and later as an adult, I had a tote, tablet, and stylus. As the latter, I appeared more sophisticated, but my reaction was the same. In both cases, I did not stand up for myself. Realizing the similarities in my reaction to being undermined both as a kid and as an adult enabled me to look deeper, understand my motives, and grow. Working with a coach, I was able to come up with an approach to articulate my concerns and needs when situations arose where I felt undermined.

Early in my career, I had a leader, Malia, whom I deeply respected. Malia often encouraged me to go to networking events. But being someone who prefers conversations with small groups of people, the thought of having to socialize amid a crowd made me hesitant, to say the least. After making the suggestion a few times, Malia admitted that she wasn't fond of networking events either—but she knew they were invaluable as they increased her visibility across the organization. She was therefore selective about which she attended but made it a priority to go to a few events every year.

Her comments led me to reflect: Did the solace of staying in my comfort zone outweigh the benefits that participating in select networking events could have on my career?

I decided to adopt Malia's strategy, attending select networking events and committing to stay there for a defined amount of time. Before each event, I would identify specific people or groups I wanted to learn about, and even thought of some discussion starters. Having a clearly defined intention and plan before the event helped mitigate my fears about not having anything compelling to say. And fully committing to attend a set number of events made each one a mini-adventure and an opportunity to explore. My underlying discomfort wore off as I started to find my groove, as it so often does once we build a habit. I began to see how in prioritizing my comfort, I had been shutting the door to new possibilities.

In chapter 3, I talked about the importance of choosing your path intentionally. Committing intentionally is just as important. If I'd decided to attend networking events without intentionally structuring my experience around my goals, I would've had a much harder time keeping my commitment. Commitment lays the foundation for growth, curiosity enables us to develop that foundation, and intentionality allows us to create the framework. When you are ready to pursue growth, and you know which direction you'd like to head, ask yourself: How can I further my goals for getting there?

Lastly, Trust Others

Whether it is teaching, mentoring, coaching, shadowing, or something else, *one of the greatest gifts afforded to mankind is the ability to learn from one another.* There's a reason I mention this point last, instead of first. Relentlessly pursuing growth requires knowing "why"—why do you want to grow? And why do you want to grow in a specific area? Without doing the hard and exciting work of seeking out these answers for ourselves, it's easy to adopt the expectations of others—our parents, our boss, our friends—and affix them to ourselves. This can lead us down the treacherous path of leading a life that's driven by the expectations of others.

> Commitment lays the foundation for growth, curiosity enables us to develop that foundation, and intentionality allows us to create the framework.

As I mentioned above, we tend to want a road map before embarking on a journey. When you insist on following a predetermined and set path, you may soon find yourself on a journey in which you miss unforeseen opportunities and are uninspired. Worse, you may end up at a destination that looks wonderful on paper but doesn't give you the sense of fulfillment you thought it would.

If you ask for advice too soon about how and where to grow, you can open yourself to undue influence—even when that influence is coming from a good place. By contrast, if you wait and seek advice when you have a clearer understanding of where you intend to go, you'll be able to ask more pointed questions that a trusted source can guide you through. Being mindlessly open to being influenced is like asking someone to give you a road map to whatever destination they recommend. Being intentional and seeking guidance, however, is like handing someone the map you're already working with and asking for specific directions.

Growth requires openness and discernment. By trusting others with your road map, you are working with curiosity and opening yourself to feedback, so it's important to be intentional about who you're leaning on and why. Keep this in mind as you decide who to trust in this process. Make sure they will have your best interests in mind. And remember, trusting someone doesn't require that you believe that everything they say is 100 percent accurate. It requires that you believe they're capable and their intentions toward you are pure, so that you can be receptive to what they have to offer.

While building your own road map may seem more challenging, it will ultimately leave you with a greater sense of control and motivation about the direction you are headed.

Reflect and Imagine …

As Kyle Carpenter, retired US Marine and Medal of Honor recipient said, "Even the smallest of steps eventually completes the grandest of journeys."[9] Indeed, all great journeys are completed one step at a time. And as we take small steps on our journey, others who might be more experienced can play a pivotal role by walking alongside us and helping us to embrace opportunities. Here's a tip that can help you to look behind the door of your potential.

Find a mentor. Finding a mentor can seem like a daunting task. It doesn't have to be. Here's a way to do it.

---

9   Kyle Carpenter, *You Are Worth It: Building a Life Worth Fighting For* (New York, NY: William Morrow & Co., 2019).

Imagine what you want your personal or professional life to entail in three to five years. How would it be different, and in what ways would it be the same?

To achieve what you hope for, what would you need? These could be skills or capabilities you'll need to build or connections you'll need to foster.

Are there gaps in what you can build yourself? Could another person help you learn new skills, develop abilities?

Think of who could help you fill those gaps. Ask them for help. If you can't think of anyone, ask others for suggestions, introductions, or recommendations.

• • •

Making the commitment to grow can be scary because it's like walking into the unknown, which unveils the possibility of failure. But sometimes, our fear of failure is so strong it undermines all the progress and plans we've made. And oftentimes, the difference between growing and treading water hinges on how we manage that fear. Could a fear of failure be hindering your progress? If so, in the next chapter you'll be able to take a closer look at why and decide what to do about it.

CHAPTER 5

Perfect Is Not on the Menu

Strive for continuous improvement instead of perfection.

—KIM COLLINS

Are you scared of the dark? What about heights? I promise I'm not about to make a pivot in this chapter into telling ghost stories or horror stories—but I do want to take a moment to talk about fear. We all experience fear in life, based in real and imagined threats to our safety. While there are plenty of times when fear keeps us protected, there are also plenty of times when this hair-raising impulse doesn't quite match the threat itself.

The American Psychological Association defines fear as "a rational reaction to a potentially dangerous event or object."[10] Fear is natural, but when it is excessive and irrational, it becomes a phobia. A phobia is defined as a "persistent and irrational fear," which is either "strenuously avoided

---

10   Heather Hatfield, "Phobia—Fear vs. Phobia," WebMD, accessed November 19, 2021, https://www.webmd.com/anxiety-panic/features/fear-factor-phobias.

or endured with marked distress."[11] Lots of common phobias are external: arachnophobia is the extreme irrational fear of spiders; claustrophobia is the extreme fear of crowded spaces. We may be familiar with these terms, but I wonder: Have you ever heard of atychiphobia? While this term may be less known, the phobia is one of the most common. The word translates to an extreme fear of failure. However, in less extreme circumstances, "perfectionism," known as the refusal to accept any standard that isn't flawless, might be the more appropriate translation.

When we fear something, we give it power over us. And if we're not careful, we can begin to make decisions that help us avoid facing our fear, rather than learn to conquer it, or put it in its place. Of course, we can't learn from something we so strenuously work to avoid. So how can we learn to unleash ourselves from the grip of perfectionism and the fear of failing?

Learning to Let Go of Perfection

One day, I was at my physical therapist's office to work on an issue I was having with mobility. The effects of MS are varied, some temporary and some permanent. One such effect is referred to as MS gait or difficulty in walking. In my case, I tended to lose balance easily and tripped often. In order to improve my walking ability, my physical therapist put me on a machine that strengthens muscles through neuromuscular magnetic stimulation. The machine was supposed to repeatedly lift and drop the top of my foot, as if to remind my foot how to move. As he readied my leg for the movements, he warned me that the machine made most people very uncomfortable. While on the machine, as I watched my foot go up and down without any effort, I couldn't help but laugh—and he was stunned by my reaction. My physical therapist later informed me that people normally dislike the machine because of the loss of control and unusual sensations it causes. Yet the lack of control

---

11   Definition of "phobia," American Psychological Association, accessed November 19, 2021, https://dictionary.apa.org/phobia.

was exactly what I found so wonderful. To me, the challenges I experienced walking revealed an imperfection. Choosing to use a machine that amplified the imperfection by taking control away from me in order to help me improve felt ironic. To get better, I had to let go.

Throughout my life, I never saw a challenge as something that would overtake me. This confidence wasn't grounded in always "winning" because I didn't always win. However, I was confident that as long as I did not accept anything less than the optimum, I could conquer anything. Filled with perfectionist tendencies, my goal was to keep everything around me under control, and thereby control the outcome of my life. Without knowing it, I was white-knuckling my way through life, driving hard to succeed, not because I was committed to my journey, but because I was intent on avoiding the terrible burn of not living up to expectation.

Looking back, I wish I would've asked myself that all-important question: *Whose expectations* am I trying to live up to? Perfectionists base their standards on the approval of others, or of society at large. The problem with doing so is that those standards are constantly changing. The inability to meet an ever-shifting bar leaves the perfectionist with a deep sense of inadequacy. There's remarkable irony in the fact that a perfectionist, despite achieving much, often feels like the biggest failure.

> There's remarkable irony in the fact that a perfectionist, despite achieving much, often feels like the biggest failure.

Attempting to Beat Vulnerability to the Punch

I may have laughed at my lack of control in the physical therapist's office that day, but just a few years earlier, the awareness of that same lack of control had me on my knees. The hardest part of receiving the diagnosis of MS was hearing that there was no cure. Without a cure, on some level my fate was no longer in my control. And without having control over my own destiny, how could I possibly overcome this challenge?

After my diagnosis, I felt out of balance: it seemed my body had gone on a loony adventure without telling my heart and my mind. At the time, the only acceptable reprieve to me was a cure. Realizing there was none, I decided to adopt a familiar method of dealing with fear, which Brené Brown refers to as "beating vulnerability to the punch."[12] For me, that entailed imagining the worst-case scenario in hopes that when the dreaded outcome surfaced, it wouldn't hurt too much, because it couldn't be as grave as what I anticipated. I began realigning my goals to help me avoid the strong feelings of loss I was experiencing. For some time, I suppressed dreams of getting married and having kids. I also avoided engaging in some cherished hobbies not because I wasn't capable but because I figured if I chose to stop when I was still capable, it meant I was in control.

My next goal was to find the "culprit." If the disease didn't have a cure, then surely it had a cause. So in addition to editing my life goals, I spent the days after receiving the news searching for a culprit. The doctors told me the condition wasn't hereditary. And while cases of MS tend to arise in colder climates, it seemed unlikely that the condition arose as a product of my upbringing in places like Italy. As I began to blame myself, the doctors quickly told me there was nothing I could've done to cause this either.

With no one else to blame, I started pointing fingers at the sky. My life crisis had morphed into a crisis of faith. After decades of relying on God, trusting that He would protect me, I felt He had done something far worse: with my diagnosis, He hadn't just abandoned me—He had shown me He wasn't even paying attention.

Every once in a while, life brings you an epiphany just when you need it most. One evening, as I was preparing a meal and reflecting on my feelings of

---

12   "The Wholehearted Life: Oprah Talks to Brené Brown," Oprah.com, May 15, 2013, https://www.oprah.com/spirit/brene-brown-interviewed-by-oprah-daring-greatly/5.

disappointment with God, I was reminded of a verse of scripture: "My grace is sufficient for you, for My power is made perfect in weakness."[13] It took me a while to unpack what this could mean in my present situation—I couldn't see how power could emerge from this weakness. But as my heart began to ponder the meaning of this verse, I realized that perhaps rather than focusing on the lack of strength, my opportunity was to focus on what my perceived weakness could teach me.

I would never refer to any illness as a "gift." At the same time, this experience proved to be a turning point in my life. During a period of reflection, I realized that while MS may have been causing a physical imbalance, the truth was I hadn't been balanced in other ways for a while. As I looked back on the last five, ten, fifteen years of my life, most of my memories involved work. Whole years seemed to be wrapped up in quick ten-minute moments when I received an accolade, award, or praise. I'd been working so hard, but toward what exactly? I didn't immediately know the answer.

The Limitations of Perfection

My MS diagnosis revealed a hidden opportunity to question what I perceived to be valuable, specifically what I was building through living and why. I realized that my commitment to perfection and fear of failure had led me to "win" many things that didn't really matter to me. I'd duped myself into thinking that my life had to fit a specific mold. And in so doing, I'd forgone the opportunity to explore the myriad of other pathways that might exist.

With God on my side, I decided to consciously get out of my comfort zone, rather than allow myself to sit in pain indefinitely. I was ready to loosen the grip on my perfectionism and find out what else was out there for me to explore. And as I started ceding some of my hard-fought-for control, giving it back to God, I fell in love with Him all over again. I began to think of God and myself as cocreators, wherein my job was neither to sit and accept whatever

---

13   2 Corinthians 12:9.

came my way nor to steer my ship completely on my own. Instead, I realized that the opportunity before me was to accept my reality and to actively work to create a life that was truly mine. A life where, when faced with a physical therapy machine that highlights my loss of control, I could laugh at my imperfections. If God's strength could shine in my weaknesses, surely I could too.

Why Perfectionism Doesn't Work

There's another irony of perfection that's worth mentioning: upholding the narrow standard of perfection is not only energy-depleting, but it also stifles growth. Aiming for perfection makes us so afraid to fail that we often refuse to try. We minimize our desires out of fear that we will not achieve them. We also try to repress our needs, convincing ourselves that our needs are unrealistic or meeting them isn't that important.

> Upholding the narrow standard of perfection is not only energy-depleting, but it also stifles growth.

Perfectionism can put a serious damper on our journey. And the innate perfectionist need to exercise control can also hurt those around us. This is yet another reason to fight off this instinct as best we can.

Perfectionism Clouds Our Reasoning

I knew a business leader who was planning to share a message about an organizational change that would make the jobs of her direct reports cumbersome. A classic perfectionist, she took great pride in and had been rewarded for her ability to execute complex operations almost flawlessly. Convinced the change would not be well received, she decided to control the dialogue by informing her direct reports of the change and immediately telling them that she knew they were not thrilled, but they needed to "just get on the bus." She then proceeded to ask if they had any questions. As would be anticipated, no one uttered a word.

After the meeting, she decided to take the better approach, which was to individually ask them to share their thoughts and concerns about the change, along with suggestions on how specific challenges could be overcome. This approach yielded better results, but the prior approach delayed progress because the trust had been broken.

This may sound like a much different story than my journey through perfectionism with MS, but at their core, they have a very similar message: when we tie ourselves to a single perfect ideal, we put on blinders that prevent us from seeing other possibilities that could result in a better outcome. The rigidity of perfection makes it hard to adapt to the real-life situation at hand and respond effectively, knowing that while the outcome may not be what we want, it can still be positive.

In Weakness, There Is Strength

Helen Keller said, "Character cannot be developed in ease and quiet. Only through experience of trial and suffering can the soul be strengthened, ambition inspired, and success achieved."

When we refuse to accept our weaknesses and mistakes, we miss the opportunity to build the inner fortitude that comes from the knowledge that we can weather any storm.

No journey is ever going to be perfect. Another irony of perfection is that acknowledging and understanding those moments in which we are imperfect brings us closer to realizing our strengths. Oftentimes, when things fall apart, there's nobody to blame,

When we refuse to accept our weaknesses and mistakes, we miss the opportunity to build the inner fortitude that comes from the knowledge that we can weather any storm.

and there might be delays, unexpected bumps to our plans, and unexpected surprises that couldn't have been predicted. But those hurdles can make the journey all the more special. A noble and attainable goal is improvement, not perfection. And improvement has no ceiling. While none of us will ever reach a perfect state, it doesn't mean we can't improve. The road to perfection is despairing, but the path of improvement is filled with the brave.

Reflect and Imagine ...

I came close to letting my desire for perfection steer me away from the pathway that was available to me, because I was afraid that accepting a lower standard would make me mediocre. However, I learned that excellence can be achieved without striving for perfection. Indeed, pursuing excellence allows one to focus on improving without fixating on perfect outcomes. Still, perfectionism isn't an easy habit to lose. As I noted in chapter 3, when I was hesitant to go on walks in daylight because others might see me fall, I was still struggling with the desire to appear flawless even years after my diagnosis. You may have to choose imperfection again and again, but take solace in the fact that the choice is yours to make. As you proceed on your journey, consider the following:

Avoid absolutes in the way you think and speak about yourself. Perfectionism often makes it seem like our lives are an all-or-nothing game. Either we're the best, or we're the worst. In reality, absolutes are never helpful in describing ourselves. As you'll learn in the next chapter, we are not finished products. So how can we claim a label when we're still growing and evolving?

Reframe your self-speech. Refrain from using absolutes and steer toward more understanding language. For example, you are not always lazy—when you are tired, you struggle to put in all of your effort. Or you are not always abrupt. When you are overwhelmed, you don't have energy to carry on conversations, so you tend to end them abruptly. By adopting this speech, you can foster a growth mindset, rather than calcify an absolutist mindset. Not labeling behaviors as qualities that define you allows you to identify behaviors you want to change and to know that you can indeed change. In addition, it enables you to be gracious toward others, acknowledging that we all make mistakes, and we are all capable of growth.

• • •

When you realize that perfection is an illusion, then you can deal with your mistakes in a manner that leads to growth, not self-chastisement. The problem is many of us are so reliant on perfectionism as a motivating force that it can be hard to figure out what to replace it with. Perhaps, just as there is strength in weakness, there are revelations to be unveiled in failures and mistakes. And perhaps those revelations are exactly what we need to liberate ourselves from the pull of perfection. Pursuing perfection will always lead one to feel inadequate because we were never meant to be perfect. We are meant to be learners and to embrace experiences as opportunities to grow and evolve.

CHAPTER 6

Get Close to Your Mistakes

The great glory in living lies not in never falling,
but in rising every time we fall.

—NELSON MANDELA

From a young age, I viewed mistakes as an enemy that needed to be strictly avoided. The fact that my MS diagnosis felt like a failure was therefore no surprise, though it's sad to think that I perceived it as such. Seeking perfection confines you to a very narrow standard of acceptance, where anything that looks different is perceived as less than. When I began loosening myself from the grip of perfectionism, I was met with an unexpected challenge: "Is an achievement worthy if it isn't perfect?"

When considering what it might take to overcome perfectionism, it's worth it to turn to the realm of phobias or irrational fears for some answers. In treating phobias, doctors often utilize exposure therapy—a treatment that exposes individuals to the things they fear and avoid while in a safe environment.[14] The theory is that by experiencing the thing they're afraid of over and over, "the thing" will eventually lose its powerful hold on the individual. With treatment, a terrifying spider can become just another house pest.

If given the choice between confronting a spider and confronting our failures, many might choose to meet the spider head-on. Admitting our mistakes and risking exposing ourselves to judgment and rejection by others can seem counterproductive. But what if getting comfortable with our mistakes is exactly what we need to do to flourish? The way we talk about our mistakes has a direct impact on how we view them. And we can talk about our mistakes in a manner that encourages growth.

A Different Way to View Mistakes

When I was searching for motivation beyond perfectionism, one approach that resonated profoundly was expressed by Simon Sinek. Sinek speaks a lot about how we grapple with failure. In one discussion, he underscored just how limiting the term "failure" can be.[15] Not only does the term have strong negative connotations, but it also implies a level of finality that doesn't often map to the circumstances at hand. Sure, projects can fail or succeed. Plans can be cut short. But how can an individual have failed, when—by nature of their very aliveness—their journey is still in progress?

Sinek suggests we reconsider how we interpret our failures and entertain a new perspective: rather than failing, we fall. It might be tempting to think these are just semantics—far from it. If failure implies an ending, falling implies the inevitable possibility of rising once again. Babies can only learn to walk by falling. Even the world's most successful athletes will fall, but their greatness lies in rising again and taking on yet another challenge. We recognize

---

14   "What Is Exposure Therapy?" American Psychological Association, July 2017, https://www.apa. org/ptsd-guideline/patients-and-families/exposure-therapy.

15   Simon Sinek, "Choose Falling Over Failure," YouTube, March 17, 2020, https://www.youtube. com/watch?v=TTMiILxqBSc.

through these examples that falling doesn't predetermine the future, and yet we struggle to apply this example to our own journeys. Why?

Sinek is one of many thinkers who articulates how limiting our concepts of failure can be. Other authors such as Carol Dweck, in her book *Mindset: The New Psychology of Success*, notes that people with a fixed mindset tend to see themselves as finished products, rather than works in progress. As such, they don't believe they can learn from the mistakes they make—instead, failure is simply a nasty mark on their record. People with a growth mindset, on the other hand, see failure as an opportunity to learn.[16]

If you can think of a time when you held a fixed or growth mindset in light of a certain outcome, you already know that a fixed mindset rarely leads to anything constructive. We learn a lot more about ourselves and the world by falling and getting back up than by coasting along or viewing our mistakes as dead ends. Unfortunately, we are often tested by the pressure to conform. Our culture has a long way to go before it admits that learning from mistakes can be more useful than "getting it right" every time. And just as it benefits us to think of our mistakes as opportunities to grow, it also benefits us to not conceal our mistakes.

The Benefit of Revealing Our Mistakes

We live in a culture that tells us our vulnerabilities make us weak. But remember in the last chapter, when I mentioned that it may just be our weaknesses that make us strong? Mistakes are inevitable. We all make them—and we all know that everyone else around us does too, whether or not we see them. Contrary to what the tendency to hide our mistakes might lead you to believe, people value witnessing moments when others err. You might be tempted to think it's just mean-spirited. There's more to it. It enables connection.

---

16   Twana Young, "Success and Failure: How Growth Mindset Can Change Education," MIND Research Institute Blog, accessed November 19, 2021, https://blog.mindresearch.org/blog/how-growth-mindset-can-change-education.

While we may admire competence, studies have shown we also tend to find it difficult to connect with those we believe are *too* competent. When we experience people who never err, we struggle to relate to them—they're not like us and are therefore unapproachable. On the other hand, when we see someone we admire make an everyday mistake, we relate to them.

Known as the Pratfall Effect,[17] this phenomenon spotlights what we already know: we humans are not each other's enemies. We are meant to be collaborators. And vulnerability is a much better tool for collaborating and learning together than perfectionism will ever be.

Excessively Reprimanding Mistakes Hinders Learning

I once worked with a manager who had very high standards. Working with her was a gift, because I learned to do things better than I would have if I didn't have her guidance. She also had high expectations. One day, after a team meeting, she stopped by my office to see how I was doing and what I thought of the meeting.

During that meeting, a client shared information about a product his team was developing from the incubation stage. I was confused by his presentation and was unsure if the misunderstanding was on my part or on his. After the meeting, when my manager asked me what I thought of the presentation, I responded in a generic manner: "It was interesting. His team is working on a promising cutting-edge product."

Unwilling to settle for my generic response, she then asked some follow-up questions, like "What's the most interesting component of what they're building, and how could we speak about this externally to generate interest?" After a few such questions, I informed her that I would like to meet

---

17   "Interesting Psychological Phenomena: The Pratfall Effect," Brescia University, June 26, 2017, https://www.brescia.edu/2017/06/pratfall-effect/.

with others in the client's organization or hear from him again, because his narrative wasn't clear to me.

I expected her to leave the conversation with a low opinion of my abilities; after all, "I should know this stuff." However, to my surprise, she said, "I felt the same way. It was hard to follow his presentation because he used very technical lingo. I don't think he realized our team needed technical concepts to be explained with an orientation toward the customer, not the developer." She also mentioned other teammates looked confused during his presentation—so she planned on inviting someone from the client's organization to explain the product further.

Needless to say, my manager's response surprised me. It was validating to know I was not sailing alone in the sea of confusion. I was originally inclined to silence myself out of fear, but her interest in my perspective and that of others revealed an opportunity that benefited the entire team. In such instances it might be easy to think we are isolated, but it's generally fair to assume when one person is confused, others are too—and speaking up gives others an opportunity to learn.

Vulnerability Propels Accountability. Accountability Drives Growth.

I learned a pivotal lesson from this experience: being vulnerable may leave us feeling exposed, but that exposure helps shed light on problems that need solving. And the sooner the light shines, the sooner you can start solving those problems.

Many of us seek to hide problems because we are fearful of others' reactions. But another reason we'd sometimes rather "fake it" is because once those problems see the light of day, we are responsible for doing something about them. *Accounten*, the root word of "accountability," means "to count." When we make mistakes, we should strive to make them count and not let the learning opportunity pass us by. *Ex causa*, the root word of "excuse," means "without explanation." If, when we make a mistake, we try to shove it under the rug, we rob ourselves of the opportunity to take any meaning or explanation from the experience.

Meanwhile, "mistake" simply means "make an error." Mistakes are by definition unintentional. Throughout this book, I have stressed—and will continue to stress—the importance of intentionality. Since mistakes are by definition unintentional, why would we define ourselves based on a set of things we never intended to do?

Don't Define Yourself or Anyone Else by Mistakes

When working with another astute senior leader of an organization, I was reminded of an important lesson: if we are not to be labeled by our mistakes, we should be careful to not label others by theirs. This leader, Jack, led an organization of over a thousand people, with a seven-person senior management team reporting directly to him. Each quarter, we held meetings with the managers to discuss the performance, growth opportunities, and financial rewards for all employees in the organization.

During one of the meetings, several managers were defensive when their team members' achievements were not recognized as superior. While their frustration was understandable—it's natural for a leader to assume that the perception of their team is a reflection on them—the lack of leadership maturity was disappointing.

After the meeting, as Jack and I recapped, he voiced his concerns at the manner in which the managers expressed their frustration. When I asked him what I could've done differently, he shared that I expressed disappointment through my body language and suggested that my response made it harder to uncover the root of the managers' concerns. While I wasn't surprised that Jack shared his candid perspective with me because we had a strong relationship, the manner in which he articulated the feedback stood out to me. He said, "The managers are scared because they don't know how to deliver bad news, and they need help. During the conversation, you expressed disappointment nonverbally, and because they're seeking approval, your response was not viewed as endearing. That fractures connection."

Upon reflecting, I realized that through Jack's candid and thoughtful feedback, he displayed the leadership that I had the opportunity to show during the meeting. His choice of words was deliberate, and instead of labeling or "punishing" me for a mistake, he held me accountable for it, sharing his perception and articulating what "better" looks like.

Reflect and Imagine ...

Perfectionism closes the doorways to learning and growth. Meanwhile, owning our mistakes opens doorways we never knew existed as we seek solutions to problems. Mysteriously, in our weakest moments often lie great opportunities; they are inflection points that propel us when we capitalize on them. Rather than stay mad or beat yourself up when you mess up, why not get curious? A creative solution might reveal new pathways on your journey's road map. The following prompts can help you get close enough to your mistakes that they propel your growth.

> Mysteriously, in our weakest moments often lie great opportunities; they are inflection points that propel us when we capitalize on them.

What's a mistake you made recently? How did you handle it?

Did you own up to it? If so, how? If you didn't own up to it, why didn't you?

What did you learn from the experience?

Would you do anything different next time?

• • •

I hope these last three chapters have inspired a desire in you to grow toward your unique passions, instead of an arbitrary standard of perfection. As you continue your journey, in addition to your travel guide filled with lessons and reminders, you might find that a few other things will benefit you— things such as essential elements that can support and strengthen you in your pursuit. In part 3, we'll take a look at those essentials and make sure you're all ready to go.

PART 3

PACK THE ESSENTIALS

CHAPTER 7

Make True Friends and Keep Them Close

Trustworthy friends are very hard to come by, and when
they do, be sure to keep them without a hesitation.

—EDMOND MBIAKA

Before we enter the next phase of your journey, I want to take a step back and reflect on where we just came from—and where we're headed next. Part 2 was all about the importance of intentional growth, the dangers of perfectionism, and the lessons that mistakes can offer us when we learn from them. Here, it's worth underscoring an important misnomer about growth: it's not always linear. In fact, sometimes growing is more like touring a building on a spiral staircase.

As Yancey Strickler, the cofounder of Kickstarter, wisely notes in his widely read blog The Ideaspace, we commonly think of time—and thus growth and progress—as a straight line, angled upward. But before the modern age, the way we moved through time was not considered to be a straight line but rather a circle. However, Strickler suggests that neither is entirely accurate: we don't progress on a straight line, nor do we endlessly circle back to the same things. Rather, the path of progress is more like an upward spiral: "We constantly circle the same themes and challenges in our lives. The past keeps echoing back. These echoes are opportunities to make better decisions and grow into more mature versions of ourselves (shifting the spiral "up") or to make *worse* decisions and regress (shifting the spiral "down").[18] He also infers that navigating time, progress, and our journey of growth "is much easier when we're *aware that the spiral exists*," because we realize that "our struggles simply mark another loop on the climb."

We all desire to zoom out the lens on our lives and see our various ups and downs like dots on a graph displaying an upward trajectory over time. So how do we create that kind of trajectory for ourselves? How can we make sure that, as we spiral toward our future, we're headed in the right direction?

That's what part 3 is all about. On any journey, what you pack can make or break your trip. How can you climb a mountain if you forget your hiking boots? Each of the next three chapters will describe a "travel essential" that can support and strengthen you—and the first of these essentials is friendship.

John Donne famously said, "No man is an island entire of itself; every man is a piece of the continent, a part of the main." Sometimes, when you find yourself in a spiraling loop that threatens to derail you from achieving your goals, what you need most is a trusted confidante who can remind you that you are not alone—that you are part of something greater, a landscape bigger than you could ever imagine. And when you're struggling to move on, a friend can offer an essential gift: a helping hand, pulling you up and out of your downward spiral.

How Will You Be Remembered?

No woman or man can thrive in isolation. Indeed, as is often said, it usually takes a village to do anything worthwhile. The value trusted friends can have in our lives and on our legacy cannot be overestimated. Trusted friends help us

---

18   Yancey Strickler, "Theories of Time," The Ideaspace, July 5, 2020, https://ideaspace.substack.com/p/theories-of-time.

stay on track by asking us how things are going, sharing suggestions on how to do better, and encouraging us in difficult times. They play a vital role by acting as our mirrors, revealing to us our strengths and the areas where we can grow.

This last paragraph likely doesn't come as a surprise to you, and yet the qualities of a great friend are better felt in the heart than understood through logical reasoning. So instead of simply listing off these great qualities, let me make it a little more personal: Who is the greatest friend you have—and what makes them so special?

One of the greatest friends I ever had was my sister Jessie. In her thirties, Jessie was an associate professor of nutrition and epidemiology at the University of North Carolina at Chapel Hill, Gillings School of Global Public Health—a public health program that is consistently ranked in the top three in the country. In her late-thirties, Jessie unexpectedly passed away from a pulmonary embolism—a blood clot in the lung.[19]

> The qualities of a great friend are better felt in the heart than understood through logical reasoning.

Jessie had an immense impact on my life. And in the days and years following her untimely death, I learned I wasn't the only one whose life was changed by the depth of Jessie's friendship. In fact, there were many others.

In addition to family and friends, many of Jessie's neighbors, students, and coworkers were present at her funeral—and many had a story to tell about the impact she had on their lives. The dean of the School of Public Health recounted stories of her own that highlighted this point: not only was my sister a brilliant woman, but she was also deeply invested in others and was

---

19   "Pulmonary Embolism," Mayo Foundation for Medical Education and Research, June 13, 2020, https://www.mayoclinic.org/diseases-conditions/pulmonary-embolism/symptoms-causes/syc-20354647.

committed to helping create a world where everyone had the opportunity to lead a fulfilling life.

In the years following her death, I frequently heard from friends or colleagues of my sister who wanted to share news she would've appreciated, or to simply connect with someone who knew how meaningful Jessie's friendship had been. On one occasion, a friend of hers was facing a tough situation at work and called me in tears. She was going through a challenge that Jessie used to help her work through, and she was missing the support and advice my sister used to impart.

On another occasion, one of my sister's friends was promoted to a dean position in a top university in California. When she contacted me to share the good news, she said, "I can't stop thinking of Jessie today, because we discussed and planned for this moment." She also said something I'll never forget: "Jessie would be so proud of me." It says a lot when someone achieves a significant personal goal and instantly connects the value of their achievement to a friend—especially when it's a friend who hasn't been with them for a long time.

Both of these instances happened over ten years after my sister had passed. Through these and many other examples, I am reminded of the unforgettable and remarkable impact one can make by being a trusted friend. When you are truly there for others like my sister was there for so many of us, your impact lasts a lifetime and far beyond.

Invest in Your Relationships

What does it mean to be a friend? This may seem like a simple question—more like something you might see written on the blackboard of an elementary school classroom than in a book geared toward inspiring your journey as an adult. But sometimes, the questions that seem the most obvious prove to be the most difficult to answer.

With an increasing consumption of technology and desire for instant gratification, another layer of complexity has been added to the term "friendship" that should make us think about what it means to be a friend. On many social media sites, "friends" are people you've "accepted" into your network with the click of a button. Today, friendship can be as easy as "reacting" to another person's post. It's so easy, in fact, that a person can quickly accumulate hundreds, if not thousands, of friends over the course of a couple years. When we receive positive reactions to posts we make online, we often bask in the warm glow of feeling seen or acknowledged. But what are we being "seen or acknowledged" for, exactly? Our true selves, or·how we want to be perceived?

Many of us invest a lot of time in our online networks—but often, that investment isn't so much about cultivating friendships as it is about crafting an image of ourselves that we want to present to the world. If the payoff for that investment was so great, the world will be filled with content and fulfilled people. Instead, our world is lonelier and less connected than ever, because as we craft our image on social media, we can inadvertently substitute the instant gratification of being "seen" by many for the lasting value of being truly known. So I can't help but wonder: What if, instead of presenting an image of ourselves in the hopes of getting admiration, we invested in others and in building true friendships?

> As we craft our image on social media, we can inadvertently substitute the instant gratification of being "seen" by many for the lasting value of being truly known.

When I reflect on the stories Jessie's friends continuously share, I see her deep investment in people as the central thread connecting them all. She cared about her loved ones' dreams and needs enough to devote her time to helping them realize those dreams. She celebrated with friends and family and listened as they shared their weaknesses and vulnerabilities, and she made them feel as though they could overcome them. She also wasn't afraid to respectfully offer a dissenting opinion and share her honest thoughts if she thought it would help.

Investing in friendships isn't as easy as a click of a button. In fact, it's the opposite. It's a commitment that can last for years, or even a lifetime. And it takes work. But the payoffs of investing in a friendship—and having a friend invest in you—are so much bigger than the warm glow of instant gratification. Allowing ourselves to be truly seen, unfiltered and vulnerable, is one of the greatest gifts we can give to each other.

If the question of what it means to be a friend is seemingly simple, then so, too, is the greatest solution to building friendship: you truly have to be a friend to make a friend. And being a friend starts with making little investments—listening, making time, being there in both the triumphant moments and in the painful ones. Your presence and impact could change someone's life. I know Jessie's life changed mine and that of so many others.

Finding Friends for Life at Work

One of the most common places to make friends is in the workplace. The pandemic shed light on the limits of a common myth that can disrupt our attempts to find and make friends, and that is the myth of work-life balance. As the pandemic persisted, our personal and professional lives fused, and the irrepressible quest for balance and meaningful connection surfaced. Our months-long period of social isolation forced us to examine and redefine what excelling at home and at work meant. And this exercise didn't allow us to neatly compartmentalize work and life; instead, it called into question what the differences were. When we dedicate eight hours of our day to our profession, are we not working and living? When we go home and have to attend to chores, are we not living and working?

What often thwarts our efforts in finding balance is the attempt to dichotomize our lives and selves into working versus living, when working and living are not mutually exclusive. In fact, we are always living and working, whether we are engaging personally or professionally. And whether we are working from an office building or from home, our personal lives are always in the background.

Given how much time we spend at work, keeping our true selves out of that picture and away from the people we meet there is unrealistic. During the pandemic, confined to our home offices, many of us were left with those faces on the Zoom, Google Meet, or Skype screens next to ours—the same faces many of us believe we must show just one side of ourselves to, our "business side," while withholding our needs, concerns, fears, and everything else that makes us full human beings.

While it may not always be possible for our jobs to be our passions, there is one element that can make even an unsustainable work situation more enjoyable: the people in your midst. The reality is we spend much of our waking hours engaging with our work teams. And if we can shift our mindset toward cultivating authentic relationships with our coworkers, our nine-to-fives will be more rewarding and satisfying.

We Are More Than Just Workers

When my sister passed away, I shared the news with my manager by telling her I wouldn't be able to work as late as I normally would. When I told her why, she broke down because she knew my sister meant a lot to me. With tears in her eyes, she told me to go home immediately and not come back until I was ready.

My manager understood that thinking of work and life as two separate categories isn't just misguided—it's bad for business. Over the years, she'd frequently remind me to use my vacation hours, and when I turned in travel expense reports that didn't include many meal purchases, she'd ask me if I was remembering to eat. She regarded me not as a worker but as a human being, whose personal and professional needs mattered. When our personal life isn't together, our work life will suffer and vice versa. The more people we have on our side who can understand how the two relate, the better.

We're often told that time is money. And it's true our time *is* valuable. But choosing to invest our time in friendships—including the friends we meet at work—can lead to a payoff far greater than anything money can buy. Friendships like those my sister cultivated can have an incredible impact that rewards both sides: it's a gift to have a friend invest in us and help us realize our dreams. And it's a gift to be able to do the same for those we love and care about, meeting them wherever they are on their journey and helping them through to the next stage.

Reflect and Imagine …

When you have a need, who do you call? And who calls you when they have a need? Who are the people in your life that don't just praise you but also have the courage to tell you when you're in the wrong? These are your true friends—and it's worth it to keep them close. Here are some powerful ways to do that.

Show appreciation. As Arianna Huffington said, "We need to widen our definition of self-care," because making time to give to others is "one of the most proven ways to boost our well-being."[20] Some simple ways to show appreciation are:

Say thank you and do so sincerely. Let your trusted friends know you care and why. While you're at it, say thank you to strangers you meet who offer nice gestures like holding the door for you, checking out your groceries, or answering your call on the customer service line. You'll be amazed at how these tiny gestures change your outlook and experience in life.

Actively support your friends. Oftentimes, the greatest support our friends need is with the little things: showing them that we see them and that we're there for them. A simple way to support your friends is to tell them what you appreciate about them and to articulate the value they provide to you. This little effort transforms the hearts of both the giver and the recipient.

• • •

---

20   Arianna Huffington, "What's Missing from Our Conversation on Self-
Care," Thrive Global, August 2, 2019, https://thriveglobal.com/stories/
why-giving-generosity-powerful-form-self-care-arianna-huffington/.

Close friendships are a primary essential on our journeys. But they're certainly not the only essential we will need. Friends help us to see the potential and possibilities in our lives—but in order for us to see these possibilities clearly, we must seek the truth for ourselves as well.

CHAPTER 8

Seek the Truth

We awaken by seeking answers in corners that are not popular.
We awaken by turning on the light inside when everything outside feels dark.

—SUZY KASSEM

In 2020, it was reported in *Travel + Leisure* magazine that the top two items that most people forget to pack on trips are phone chargers and toothpaste.[21] These are also items that most of us would consider essential, yet many of us can probably remember packing less "critical" items such as extra clothes and shoes for a trip. Ironically, clothes and shoes also weigh more than a phone charger and a tube of toothpaste, and they can weigh us down when we're traveling.

The same can happen on our life journey. Here, the items that can "weigh us down" are often not things we can hold in our hands or pack in our bags. They are not physical baggage but emotional baggage. I'm talking about our beliefs: the ideas, concepts, and ways of thinking we've adopted to help us frame our experiences and write our personal narratives. Oftentimes, because we've let these beliefs define who we are, questioning them or letting

---

21   Jessica Plautz and Madeline Diamond, "The Most Common Items People Forget to Pack," *Travel + Leisure*, December 3, 2020, https://www.travelandleisure.com/travel-tips/packing-tips/forgotten-items-packing-list.

them go can be very difficult. Unfortunately, some beliefs have an uncanny knack for distorting reality, obscuring the important shades and nuances of our experiences.

What is true, and how do I know it is true? These are two common questions we grapple with when we receive messages from others. Sometimes, deciphering the truth or interpreting messages can boggle our minds, because to see and accept the truth often requires that we resist the tendency to only see what we wish and hear what we like. However, in order to grow, it is often necessary to engage in behaviors we might find uncomfortable or feel inept at, such as considering perspectives that are different from ours, questioning our own beliefs, or debating with others. In spite of the discomfort these actions might arouse, they are worthwhile because they reveal the truth, and the truth can propel you. As you proceed on your journey of discovering and giving what only you uniquely can, ensuring that what you carry propels you rather than pulls you down is critical.

> To see and accept the truth often requires that we resist the tendency to only see what we wish and hear what we like.

For this wonderful journey you're on, in addition to making true friends and keeping them close, what if you also released your preconceived notions and packed something way more valuable: the unfiltered and unvarnished truth?

Why Do We Believe What We Believe?

What we believe has a profound impact on our lives, because what we believe ultimately influences what we do. But our beliefs are not always objective; they're not always based on truths.

I have what many would describe as an unrealistic fear of dogs. My reaction when a dog walks toward me is similar to how many might react if they saw a tiger on the street. Despite several attempts by friends to familiarize me with their dogs, I still hold on to a belief that dogs want to hurt me because as a kid, I was chased by a friend's dog who was ironically named Lady. This experience led me to develop a fear that I never dealt with, so to this day, my fear of dogs prevents me from participating in certain activities. This tends to be the case when we allow our fears to dictate our beliefs. And this happens with our desires as well. When we desire something, we might only see the benefits and remain closed to the downsides or the alternatives.

Our desires and fears are two forces that often stand in the way of us seeing and accepting the truth, because they lead us to perceive and label things as either positive or negative. And our perceptions can crystallize into beliefs and determine what we view as opportunities or as barriers. By examining and knowing why we hold certain beliefs, we're better able to make decisions that truly serve us.

The Mental Gymnastics of Belief

As I shared in the example above, over the years, I've held on to a belief that dogs want to hurt me. While I am intellectually aware of the companionship and protection dogs offer to others, my belief prevents me from seeing their amazing qualities.

Our brains can play a lot of mental gymnastics to form and hold a belief. And by the time we've formed one, we often find ourselves ignoring crucial information that would help us see the truth of the situation.

In an article entitled "Why Do People Believe Things That Aren't True?"[22] author and psychologist David B. Feldman highlights three "mental shortcuts" we all take to help us understand the world. Each can lead us to hold incorrect beliefs:

---

22   David Feldman, "Why Do People Believe Things That Aren't True?" *Psychology Today*, May 12, 2017, https://www.psychologytoday.com/us/blog/supersurvivors/201705/why-do-people-believe-things-aren-t-true.

1. The first mental shortcut is the tendency to look for information that confirms what we already believe while ignoring other factors. This is known as "confirmation bias." An example of this in action is: if you believe your neighbors don't value your presence, you might focus on the times when you were excluded from events and ignore the times when you were invited. And this reinforces your belief that your presence isn't valued.

2. The second is the tendency to overestimate the frequency of events based on recent memories. This is called the "availability heuristic." Many of us might be able to think of moments when we've used this mental shortcut to make decisions. I think of my mother who refuses to visit islands because of two tragic events that happened on popular tourist islands several years ago and were heavily covered in the news. Now, she believes any island vacations are a risky endeavor.

3. The third mental shortcut is called "emotional reasoning." It occurs when we draw conclusions about a situation based on how we feel, rather than the facts at hand. An example of this is the popular phrase: "That's just how I feel." This phrase is often used to defend a belief, and the rationale is centered on one's feelings. As Feldman notes, however, "feelings are just feelings," and even when they are powerful, "they can sometimes lie to us." If you've ever driven down a street and thought "I'm terrified … I know something terrible *will* happen here," then turned around and took the longer route, you know the power emotional reasoning can have on your decision-making.

As with many things, the line that separates what's good and bad can be very thin. As in the example above, it might be prudent to turn around and take an alternate route if you believe you're at risk. After all, it's a judgment call, and the downside of taking the longer route might be negligible. However, when mental shortcuts determine our major beliefs, it's worth examining our beliefs because what we learn about them will benefit us. You might find that something you've long held to be true is limiting your potential. Or you may find that some of your beliefs are grounded in truth and are worth holding on to. As Anton Chekhov said, "Man is what he believes." By asking ourselves "Why is this true for me?" we aren't just examining our thought patterns—we're also learning about ourselves, and that's vital for growth.

When we step back and ponder why we hold specific beliefs, we realize that it was a choice we made. And because the choice is ours, we can choose to adopt a different story for ourselves, one underpinned with beliefs that serve us rather than stand in our way.

See Clearly and Don't Ignore the Details

Several years ago, a friend sent a picture of her newborn to me. After telling her that her baby was absolutely beautiful, I remarked on how bright the weather was. My friend said the weather was actually quite dull, but a filter was applied on the picture, so it looked vivid. In an instant, a cloudy sky appeared bright!

While looking at filtered images can be entertaining, viewing our lives through filters can be problematic. Seeking the truth requires us to explore all sides of a situation, understanding the good and the bad so that we can form opinions based on a holistic perspective. But when we're accustomed to a specific filter, it can be difficult to appreciate

Seeking the truth requires us to explore all sides of a situation, understanding the good and the bad so that we can form opinions based on a holistic perspective.

another perspective. We might be inclined to focus solely on the positive or on the negative. And we might only hear what appeals to us or choose to believe only that which is pleasing to us.

When we consider why we cling to one perspective and struggle to entertain others, we often find that we are hanging on to comfort and resisting fear. It's comfortable to view situations in ways that appeal to us because it gives us a sense of assurance that everything will work out just the way we want it to. In contrast, paying attention to the looming warning signs or contradictions in our environment can be scary, and we might have to do something about it. But if we want to live a fulfilling life and give what we uniquely can, we need to see the truth. And it's worth remembering that this benefits not just us but also our families, friends, coworkers, and many others.

Seeing and Reading the Fine Print

Several years ago, a friend of mine who worked for a multinational company told me of an experience that happened in her workplace. A female employee was approached by several male colleagues to engage in inappropriate relationships. Multiple investigations later showed that several other female employees were also approached by the same men with the same proposition. Even worse, the men used an app to rate the appearance of their female colleagues— and they used it on the company network! Clearly there was a problem in the workplace. Once the investigations were complete, the objective was to identify what could have been done to prevent this or catch it sooner.

Several leaders took responsibility and were distressed that this happened under their watch. Upon reflecting, they acknowledged there had been warning signs that they ignored. The culture was very male dominated, many women had resigned, and those who stayed often said they felt silenced and didn't feel their opinions mattered. While it might have been tempting for those leaders to ignore the signs of a problematic workplace culture, like the fine print on a document, those signs carried a lot of weight.

You might think this story is an anomaly, but consider this: a Gallup study in 2020 showed that 45 percent of American workers experienced discrimination and/or harassment in the past year.[23] If discrimination is such a pervasive problem, why do experiences like this still occur for extended periods of time?

Like individuals, organizations crave positive feedback about their culture and what they offer. And given how difficult it is to change a culture, it can be tempting to ignore perspectives that suggest a change is needed and improvements are warranted. But just like individuals, organizations have to read the fine print in order to improve. For individuals and organizations, seeing and accepting the truth might mean removing an element of comfort, but in return you'll get something much greater: an expanded and realistic view of yourself and of your opportunities.

> Seeing and accepting the truth might mean removing an element of comfort, but in return you'll get something much greater: an expanded and realistic view of yourself and of your opportunities.

Reflect and Imagine ...

Today, society seems to place more value on being liked than on doing what is right. This can make it difficult to seek the truth, especially if it's not what we or others want to hear or see. Yet viewing situations clearly from multiple perspectives and making decisions grounded in truth are essential for growth. As you continue on your journey, here are some ideas to help you see clearly.

Examine your beliefs. We often form beliefs based on thoughts and ideas, which may be true or false. Growth often requires releasing false beliefs that we hold. And to release false beliefs, it's important to know what they are and why we hold them.

---

23   "Build a Culture Where Every Employee Can Use Their Voice," Gallup, November 8, 2021, https://www.gallup.com/workplace/215939/diversity-inclusion.aspx.

Remember Lady, my friend's dog who chased me when I was a kid? That experience led me to conclude that all dogs want to hurt me. Well, I later learned there was a good reason why Lady chased me. On the day she chased me, I was playing hide and seek with my friend at her home. While we were playing, I ran behind Lady's doghouse to "hide." When I did that, she perceived me as a threat because she'd given birth to puppies the night before, so she chased me. The reality is Lady was more interested in protecting her young than in hurting me. And that maternal instinct is a beautiful thing. If I had this context then, I might have not developed this seemingly unshakeable fear of dogs. *In seeking the truth, context matters.*

What is a strong belief that influences many of your decisions?

Is this belief based on others' opinions or an experience?

How does this belief affect your behavior? What do you do or avoid as a result of this belief?

How can you test this belief? Reading, discussing with others?

Lean on your friends. Trusted friends can often see situations we're in clearer than we can, especially if they're further removed. And we can benefit greatly from their perspectives. Next time you're wrestling with a situation personally or professionally, share with a friend. And let them know you value their perspective and want to hear it, even if it conflicts with yours.

• • •

In the last chapter, I highlighted the importance of investing in great friendships. Just like it takes time to build trust, it can also take time to examine our beliefs and change them if they're not serving us. To stay grounded in your journey, the third essential you'll need is a healthy dose of confidence. In the next chapter, we'll explore just that.

CHAPTER 9

Gain Confidence

The tests we face in life's journey are not to reveal our weaknesses but
to help us discover our inner strengths. We can only know how strong
we are when we strive and thrive beyond the challenges we face.

—KEMI SOGUNLE

When is the last time someone asked you how you were doing? Can you remember how you responded? For such a general question, it seems like we could answer in a thousand ways. But if you're like most people, you may think there's just one universally acceptable answer: "I'm doing great."

Many of us feel pressured to "have it all together"—so much so that when we're asked how we're doing, we wonder if the person asking really wants an honest answer. We also question whether it's wise to respond truthfully, especially since our worries could be misconstrued as weaknesses and our struggles misinterpreted as flaws.

Now, I am certainly not advocating for a world in which we bare the deepest parts of our soul to everyone who smiles at us in greeting. However, I believe that when our vulnerabilities are hidden from the light, they can begin to thrive in the dark. Instead of being incorporated into a healthy sense of self, our vulnerabilities can become a "dirty little secret" that we must never expose. In reality, we all hold these tender secrets that we tend to hide behind "masks."

Many vulnerabilities stem from a key question that I posed in earlier chapters: "Am I enough?" Our vulnerabilities can also stem from other fears or mistakes. And at times, it can seem like everyone else has it all together, and we're the odd ones out!

Simply put, there's no such thing as living in a permanent state of "having it all together." So the question is: What does it take to be ourselves and to live "mask-free" in a world where it's tempting to amass a collection of "masks" with a fitting one for each occasion? It starts with a healthy dose of self-confidence.

Of all the must-have essentials I've discussed, confidence is the one we're most often tempted to pretend we already have, while feeling totally overwhelmed at the thought of actually building it. This is because having and displaying confidence is the ultimate balancing act: too little confidence makes you feel inadequate and unable to reach your potential. And too much confidence falsely convinces you that you're almost perfect, thereby limiting your ability to grow. Both of these extremes prevent us from seeing the truth. It's no question finding the right balance is a tricky thing. This chapter will help you build confidence in a healthy and sustainable way.

The Limitations of Low Self-Esteem

Has someone ever complimented you or requested a favor from you, and you responded by brushing it off or downplaying your abilities? Given that many of us have either responded like this or experienced others do so, it's worth reflecting on what drives this kind of response.

Several ingrained beliefs that we hold about ourselves come from our past. And sometimes we rely on those memories as the lone predictor of what our future will look like, telling ourselves that our past failures and mistakes have etched our future in stone. The problem with this line of thinking is humans evolve, and our past is often neither representative of what we're capable of right now nor an adequate predictor of our future capabilities.

Past mistakes do not account for the lessons we've learned since we made them, or all the ways we've grown in light of our experiences. In day-to-day moments, it's easy to acknowledge that we're not the same person we were ten years ago, five years ago, or even six months ago. But sometimes, when we

> Humans evolve, and our past is often neither representative of what we're capable of right now nor an adequate predictor of our future capabilities.

face a new challenge, we look to our past mistakes as the key indicator of who we are and what we're capable of.

Consider a time in your life when someone asked you to help them with something you weren't confident you could do. Upon reflection, you might find that the request was made because that person saw something in you that you didn't see in yourself. Trusting in our abilities—including the ability to learn and improve—is essential to having self-confidence. When we don't trust in our abilities, not only do we tend to offer less, sometimes, we end up offering nothing at all.

Many researchers have studied the connection between self-confidence and personal growth, and the conclusions they've made are not surprising. Individuals with a low sense of confidence tend to be risk averse: they speak up less in meetings, they don't apply for promotions, and they let their fear of rejection guide their actions.[24] They also have a hard time accepting positive

---

24   "How Low Self-Esteem Can Cost You the Job," *Forbes*, July 22, 2010, https://www.forbes. com/2010/07/22/confidence-job-satisfaction-interview-techniques-forbes-woman-leadership-self-esteem.html?sh=40c132266c49.

feedback and choose to focus on their perceived weaknesses, rather than on their possible strengths.[25]

Low confidence can lead us to shut doors that could've led to amazing opportunities. And yet building confidence can seem overwhelming, especially if you don't know your superpowers. Luckily, two things you'll need to grow your confidence are already packed in your essentials: you need great friends who you trust, and you need to be able to see your situation clearly, without filters that suggest you're in a worse or better position than you really are.

Don't Be Afraid to Take a Risk

Even if society suggests that we're better off hiding our vulnerabilities and keeping them to ourselves, we know deep down we cannot thrive in isolation. In her book *Daring Greatly*, Brené Brown writes, "If we can share our story with someone who responds with empathy and understanding, shame can't survive."[26] Indeed, viewing situations without filters and seeing the truth about ourselves and what we're capable of is often more than a one-person job. In the confines of our own heads, low confidence can make us flail between those familiar extremes of being a superhero or being a coward. Our trusted friends know that we display signs of both, and they can support us as we take the leap into whatever endeavors we choose to pursue.

During the pandemic, many people faced unexpected challenges and encountered risks that they never imagined they'd have to. This unexpected time in history has been heartbreaking to witness; it has also given us countless stories of individuals who struggled through those challenges and came out stronger and better, thanks in no small part to the people who helped them along the way. These stories demonstrate not only the power of perseverance

---

25   Mayo Clinic Staff, "Self-Esteem Check: Too Low or Just Right?" Mayo Foundation for Medical Education and Research, July 14, 2020, https://www.mayoclinic.org/healthy-lifestyle/adult-health/in-depth/self-esteem/art-20047976.

26   Brené Brown, *Daring Greatly: How the Courage to Be Vulnerable Transforms the Way We Live, Love, Parent, and Lead* (New York: Avery Publishing, 2015).

and confidence but also the power we get when we lean on those we love and trust. In fact, I can think of no greater example of this than my own sister, At Ford.

At is a senior portfolio advisor, financial advisor, a wife, and a mother to two teenage children. During the pandemic, she decided to pursue a certification that is highly beneficial in her role and difficult to attain. And since the certification is not required, it is possessed by relatively few in the industry. The certification takes on average two years to complete, but she chose to complete it in just five months, so she could prioritize her other obligations. Her preparation for the certification was grueling. Combined with her regular work, her studies had her pulling off seventeen-hour days, seven days a week, leaving room for little else.

My sister chose to compress her certification schedule so that she would be able to spend more time with her family in the long run: five months of hard work is a lot shorter than two years of having to balance work, study, and everything else. But during those long, hard hours, my sister faced many moments of stress and self-doubt about whether she would succeed. Through it all, however, I noticed At did something powerful: she never struggled alone.

She shared her struggles, concerns, disappointments, fears, and triumphs. She intentionally chose who she shared with—she was looking to receive support from a compassionate few, rather than to have her goals trivialized, which could encourage her to give up. She was also very honest with her husband and kids about the challenges she faced and the support she would need. Her vulnerability encouraged them to do more to support the family, with her daughter cooking meals on some days, her son taking on more chores, and her husband adjusting his schedule so he could take on more responsibility at home.

Steadfast, she succeeded in getting her certification in five months, which brought her immense joy. She recognized that the help she received along the way reinforced her confidence in her capabilities and ultimately enabled her to sacrifice short-term happiness for long-term satisfaction.

When asked why she decided to pursue her certification in such a short time, At simply said she believed it was possible and knew the additional expertise would enable her to meet more needs. Specifically, it would enable her to help businesses and retirees who had an uphill battle to remain stable as a result of the pandemic. So she gave it a shot. With the certificate in hand, At was like a child who gets a renewed sense of awe when she receives a bigger Lego set because she realizes that with the additional pieces, she can build more complex structures. She exuberantly leveraged the new tools in her toolkit that the certification granted her.

Confidence and taking smart risks can create a virtuous cycle: the more we dare and succeed, the greater confidence we will have. My sister took a risk, and by leaning on others, she succeeded in gaining both new knowledge and a healthy dose of confidence that will enable her to put the knowledge to use.

It can be tempting to allow past experiences, or other people's opinions, determine how you view yourself. And when you're not feeling confident, it seems there's never a shortage of bad memories or faulty opinions to keep you feeling inadequate—and to prevent you from putting your unique gifts to use. The world has an abundance of needs but not enough people to meet them. Your friends can help you channel your inner superhero to meet some of those needs.

Confidence Is Not Arrogance

Sometimes, we shy away from expressing confidence because we do not want to be viewed as arrogant. But this fear is yet another way of looking at the world through a filter that distorts our view. Confidence and arrogance could not be more different from one another. When we are confident, our trust in our self-worth allows us to show up authentically and ask for the help we need regardless of how we may be perceived. Also, when we are confident, we don't compare ourselves with others, and our values remain consistent, regardless of the audience.

However, insecurity and fear lie at the heart of an arrogant attitude. And arrogance is often manifested when we think or say our weaknesses represent who we are, and others should just learn to deal with it. On the other hand, when we are truly confident, we accept our weaknesses. And we recognize that always feeling confident amid life's ups and downs is unrealistic. In fact, we might display self-confidence in one situation and act out of self-doubt in others. This is not an inconsistency—it's a natural tendency.

When we don't get what we aim for, it can seem like a negative spotlight has been shone on us, exposing our weaknesses for the world to see. It's hard to not fear that others will look down on us. But with a confident mindset, we know that a dark moment, no matter how negative it may seem, is not a reflection of all we can give or of who we are. We are therefore able to acknowledge our fears, face them, and overcome them.

> With a confident mindset, we know that a dark moment, no matter how negative it may seem, is not a reflection of all we can give or of who we are.

Reflect and Imagine ...

We all experience self-doubt, and sometimes it can hold us back from pursuing our dreams. Next time those doubts come lurking, here are some things to consider that can help you build confidence that is deep, authentic, and meaningful.

What is a goal you met that seemed unattainable? Perhaps you started a challenging health routine, built a key skill, or initiated a tough conversation.

What fears did you have before you started? Did you ignore, minimize, or fixate on those fears?

What did you learn about yourself from the experience?

If it were today, what would you do differently? Would you take greater risks or play it safer?

Remember your dreams. Perhaps review an old journal or recall your goals from years past. What's a dream you went after and realized? What fears did you face to move forward?

Now, consider your life today. What is a specific dream you want to chase but are hesitant? What is one thing you can do today to get closer to realizing your dream? Keep in mind that when chasing a dream, every intentional step brings you closer.

• • •

In part 3, we explored how key essentials—trusted friends, the truth, and confidence—can help steer you toward the right path as you continue on your journey. And I hope you feel energized by how much support is available to you. Now, in part 4, we'll look at the specific tools you'll need to stay the course—whatever challenges may come your way.

PART 4

STAY YOUR COURSE

CHAPTER 10

Think Right

As you think, so shall you become.

—BRUCE LEE

At this point in your journey, you may be thinking a couple different things. Perhaps you're saying to yourself, "I remember my dreams, and I see opportunities emerging, so how can I make all of them a reality?" Or perhaps you're thinking, "Oh my goodness ... I have so much on my plate right now, and I can't imagine taking on more." Both of these reflections are natural and rational. And yet both assume that growth and pursuing a dream is an all-or-nothing affair.

We often believe that pursuing and realizing our dreams requires a complete and immediate 180-degree turn from where we've been toward where we're headed. In reality, the process of growing and changing is iterative. No matter where you are at this point in your journey, you've already done some serious work. And even if the framework of your life looks the same—same job, same relationships, same city—I hope you're starting to notice how little changes to your thinking can make a big difference in the choices you make and in your life experience. Houses and other structures are often described as having "good bones." This tends to apply to the construct of our lives as well. So the goal is not to burn the "house" down, or in this case dismantle your life and rebuild it from scratch. It's to start working with what you have—the "good bones" that structure your life—and consider how you might improve your life by making little changes, like a fresh coat of paint or better carpeting does to a house.

In part 3, I shared key essentials we need to grow: true friends, a clear understanding of the truth, and a healthy dose of confidence to propel you toward your greatest desires. In part 4, I want to share a few more gems that will enable you to chase your dreams amid the life you're already living right now. That's what staying your course is all about—knowing the direction in which you're headed and getting what you need so that you can continue along the right pathway.

> Actions are manifestations of thoughts that are conceived in the mind.

Indeed, the first place where change needs to happen is in our minds. Actions are manifestations of thoughts that are conceived in the mind. We all know of someone whose thoughts played out in reality, either positively or negatively. For instance, studies have shown[27] that patients with an optimistic mindset frequently have better health outcomes than those who hold a negative outlook. We might think of this as a creepy phenomenon—or perhaps it is an exciting possibility to directly influence the outcome of our lives.

The truth is the way we think profoundly affects all aspects of our lives. I have hinted at this theme in nearly every chapter thus far, from discussing the importance of recognizing our inner superhero to highlighting the perils of perfectionism. In this chapter, however, I want to talk about the importance of mindset as it pertains to your life journey. What are your desires and

---

27   "Optimism and Your Health," Harvard Health, May 1, 2008, https://www.health.harvard.edu/heart-health/optimism-and-your-health.

intentions? What do you accept or refuse? And perhaps most importantly, who and what are you letting influence your answers to these questions?

Sometimes, the actions we take can lead us down the path of remorse—but more often, our regrets are rooted in the actions we didn't take, and the mindsets we let hold us back from pursuing our dreams. Not following our dreams often leads to a life of regret and one enmeshed in an endless series of what-ifs. Training our minds to think right is essential—and it all starts with recognizing our own power to influence and knowing what influences us.

> Not following our dreams often leads to a life of regret and one enmeshed in an endless series of what-ifs.

The Way We Think Influences the Way We Act

In chapter 7, we discussed how true friends can have a big impact on our lives, and in chapter 8, we explored the impact our beliefs have on our actions. In this chapter, I want to highlight the connection between these concepts by underscoring the importance of influence—both what influences us, as well as what we ourselves have the power to influence through our behavior. You see, one of the ways we inadvertently hold ourselves back is by adopting the mindset that what we do doesn't really matter because "what's going to happen is going to happen." In reality, *every action we take has the capacity to make a difference on our lives or on the lives of others. And when we don't recognize this, we not only sell ourselves short, but we can also inadvertently hurt others through our actions or inaction.*

Recognizing the Power You Have

We often associate power with physical prowess, but there's another type of power that we each hold, and that's the ability to make a positive or negative impact by influencing others. But sometimes, it can be difficult to recognize that we have this power—and when we don't know that we possess it, we limit ourselves.

I learned this firsthand early in my career at a team meeting with peers who managed different client accounts. During the meeting, our leader introduced a change in our client engagement process. The change was well received by most of the team because it would simplify our jobs. But a peer voiced strong opposition to the new process, stating that her client would reject it, and she suggested a different course. Notably, that peer's client led an organization that had a major impact on the company's profitability, and her client's opinion carried significant weight. However, the other team members strongly opposed her perspective, stating their clients would be disadvantaged if we pursued the course she suggested. The conversation quickly became heated, and I didn't have a strong preference for either process, so I was mostly silent.

> True leaders are not defined by a title. Leadership is demonstrated through acts of courage: speaking up and acting with a keen focus on the advancement of the whole.

After the meeting, I returned to my office puzzled by the tenor of the meeting but relatively unbothered until my manager walked into my office and asked me how I thought the meeting went. I shared my perspective and expressed sympathy for the peer whose opinion was not well received. My manager proceeded to tell me that in the meeting she was surprised I did not speak up and encourage others to be more open-minded, given that my perspectives were valued by the team. She also suggested ways in which I could have added more value.

During that conversation, I learned a key lesson: there is a difference between your role and your job. My job was to meet the client's business needs and manage the process flow. But my role on my team was to lead by assessing different perspectives, sharing insights, and advocating for different voices to be heard. In my role, the greatest value I could provide was to use my influence to shape better outcomes.

As a result, I resolved to not downplay my opportunity to contribute but rather to seize opportunities to influence and make a positive impact. I also learned a pivotal lesson about leadership. True leaders are not defined by a title. Leadership is demonstrated through acts of courage: speaking up and acting with a keen focus on the advancement of the whole. In fact, the way we see ourselves and our understanding of our role in any situation often determines how we respond. Assuming a spectator role in that meeting held me back from leveraging the opportunity I had to make a positive impact. How might your mindset be holding you back, and what might you do to shift your mindset and unleash your power?

You Have a Platform ... Who's On It?

We often think of platforms as a privilege that is bestowed upon celebrities because of the elevated level of interest they've acquired due to extraordinary talents and skills. We might say a celebrity has a huge platform because they have a wide span of influence, usually meaning a considerable number of fans and connections. You might even hear a baker say, "If I can get my chocolate chip cookies featured on Oprah's Favorite Things List, my cookies will fly off the bakery stands." And that's because the baker assumes many would buy her cookies if Oprah said she likes them, because they value Oprah's opinion. We often say the same of other celebrities, and it begs the question: Is the gift of a platform only afforded to public figures, or can anyone have a platform? Can anyone influence and make an impact?

Consider a coworker whose ideas are often endorsed by others and eventually implemented, or a neighbor whose ideas are frequently adopted at homeowners association (HOA) meetings. You may be that coworker or neighbor, or perhaps your span of influence is just limited to your three best friends. The reality is unless you've effectively avoided contact with any other human being for an extended period of time, you influence someone's perspectives and behaviors.

Now, the names or faces of people who you influence might be coming to mind, and as they do, you may feel a sense of responsibility. That's a good thing, because we are responsible for our impact and need to be mindful of how we use our platform. To better clarify this point, I want to share a special experience I had with a friend. Many years ago, I was visiting a friend from work, and she began narrating a story that both baffled and delighted me. She shared that she had been sober for a year, and to celebrate her sobriety, she decided to purchase two tickets for a Jay-Z concert, and she requested I join her. I was honored, and we made plans to attend the concert.

When we arrived at the arena the day of the concert, the energy was irrepressible, and the excitement was palpable. As soon as Jay-Z hit the stage, everyone in my line of sight got on their feet cheering, chanting, and singing along with him. Regardless of your perception of Jay-Z, one thing was undeniable that evening: he had mastered the art of influencing his audience. As he stood before us on his platform stage, we all felt we were right there with him. Except, of course, we weren't. The only ones actually allowed on Jay-Z's platform were his band, his opening act, his security team, and himself. The audience had to stay behind a clear boundary demarcating Jay-Z's space and ours. However, this boundary didn't detract from his performance—in fact, it enhanced it. Without the threat of the crowd invading his space, he could focus on what he does best: make great music and entertain.

Jay-Z, or any other artist for that matter, doesn't need to apologize for not letting their fans up on their stage, and fans don't expect them to. The boundaries artists erect around their performing platforms, and the intentional decisions they make around whom they allow to join them on stage, are vital for their performance and safety—and their fans are happier for understanding their own constraints. You see, it's easy for performers to guard their platforms, and most of us understand why they do so. Why then does it feel so hard, sometimes, for us to do the same?

If Jay-Z let even one fan on stage with him, he'd cede much of his control to the whims of this individual enjoying his time in the limelight. And he'd have to contend with the impact that would have on his safety and on the experience of others at his concerts. In our lives, it's not so different: the cost of allowing the wrong person onto our platforms is high, because they can and will influence how we think (our headspace) and how we feel (our heart-space). This approach, which many celebrities adopt, led me to wonder why so many of us allow uninvited people to stand on our "platform stage" and take control. It also led me to ponder a series of questions that I would encourage you to consider: Who influences my thoughts and actions? Is everyone or anyone able to alter my message and self-image? And if others surface onto my platform unwelcomed, how do I respond?

You see, others can try to get onto our platforms in every area of our lives, but we get to decide who stays there. While letting others in and seeking other perspectives is critical for growth, before we allow someone to influence our way of thinking, it's important to consider the impact they'll have on our lives. Of course, diligence does not guarantee that we'll always make the right decisions, but thoughtfully deciding who influences us will enable us to make better decisions. And when we do make mistakes, by understanding what drove our actions and committing to doing better, we can let our mistakes propel us rather than hold us back.

As I wrote at the beginning of this chapter, this part of your journey is all about making beneficial changes, not unnecessarily altering the fabric of your life. When you think right and seize opportunities to make improvements, even small ones, you may be surprised how much these simple steps can improve your life.

Reflect and Imagine ...

When we face opportunities and challenges, it's important to know what we are seeking, how we think we can meet our needs, and what assumptions are steering our thoughts—including our various influences and influencers. And as we make decisions, it's helpful to remember that our actions and intentions have an effect and impact beyond our realization.

Know what you are truly seeking. Many times, before we pose a question, we have an expectation of what the answer will or should be. And this sometimes leads us to make decisions prematurely. To avoid this, it is helpful to truly understand what you are seeking and why. For example, rather than asking yourself "Should I get a new X (a new job, join a new group, etc.)?" perhaps ask, "What do I like about X? How is it propelling me? How is it holding me back?" With each question you ask, new ideas will be unlocked. This will enable you to better understand what you truly desire.

Consider various ideas—even "bad" ones. It's easy to make decisions by discounting ideas that we think are dumb or unrealistic without truly evaluating them. And when we do so, we often rob ourselves of the opportunity to consider all of our options. But sometimes, knowing what doesn't work helps us to find what *will* work. Going back to the example above of wanting to leave a situation such as a job, ask yourself the following: Other than leaving my job *now*, what would make my time here worthwhile? Learning a new skill? Taking on other additional responsibilities? Taking on less responsibilities? Modifying my work schedule?

• • •

As you start to change your life from the inside out, thinking right will prove a crucial resource. But as you begin to flex your decision-making muscles, I hope you remember that sometimes the right decision isn't to push forward but to walk away. Sometimes, sticking around a bad situation is what we come to regret most. In the next chapter, we'll learn more about why this is an important lesson and how you can begin to apply it to your life.

CHAPTER 11

Know When to Walk Away

You will never achieve what you're capable of if you're too
attached to things you're supposed to walk away from.

—UNKNOWN

I've always enjoyed bouquets of flowers, but I admit that over the years I've also found them rather tricky to maintain. Maybe you can relate: If you're like me, when you receive a beautiful bouquet, you gratefully place it in a striking part of your home, so you can be reminded of the special occasion or person that the gift represents. For the first week, the flowers bloom vibrantly, their aroma filling the room with an alluring fragrance. But after some time, they naturally begin to wilt: their aroma, once sweet, turns stale, and their beautiful colors fade to dull brown. After a certain point, no amount of clean water or fertilizer will rejuvenate their fading stems, and you realize it's time to throw them out.

A browning bouquet on our tables offers us a stark reminder of when it's time to say goodbye to those once sweet-smelling buds. If only it were this easy to tell when other things in our lives have overstayed their welcome!

Unlike flowers, we humans have the option to move and plant ourselves in new environments that allow us to thrive. For many reasons, however, be it fear, insecurity, or an attachment to that which is familiar, we often pass up these opportunities for exploration and growth. Instead, we choose to stay in environments in which we wilt and lose our spark. Eventually, we may even lose our ability to bloom at all.

Forrest Gump famously said life is "like a box of chocolates." For me, life is like a bouquet of flowers: when we stop blooming, it's time to make a change. But you might not be able to rely on the visual of a wilting bouquet to tell you when you need to move in a different direction. So in this chapter, I hope to equip you with some tools that can help you determine whether you're blossoming or wilting, and what you can do about it. After all, on this journey of growth, the choice is yours to make!

Why Is It So Hard to Walk Away?

Ironically, walking away from a situation that doesn't serve us—whether it's a job, an environment, or a relationship—can be incredibly challenging. And yet, we all make the decision to walk away several times a day, often without much thought. If a grocery store doesn't have an item we're looking for, we leave and check out another one. If a fitness program isn't delivering the results we want, we change it up. We are all familiar with "walking away," but when it seems the consequence of a decision could affect our lives profoundly, we might feel overwhelmed and unable to make a decision, even one we know we should.

Indeed, when it comes to the big things in life, deciding whether to walk away can feel like a minefield of paradoxes: First, quitting can feel like you're avoiding commitment, yet physically remaining in a place that your heart has left can indicate the very same thing. Second, quitting can feel like you're weak and "giving up" or don't have long-term vision, yet remaining in place can also mean you're giving up on yourself by staying in your comfort zone! Some say, better the devil you know than the one you don't. Others say, when one door closes, another one opens. What, if anything, can make navigating this minefield any easier?

If "quitting in good conscience" were a college course, there would be some serious prerequisites needed to prepare you. Seeking the truth, resisting the lure of perfectionism, and gaining confidence all play a role in making the decision to walk away more lucid, though not necessarily easier. Perhaps most importantly, without knowing yourself, you'll never know all that's in you and what you can aim for.

> Without knowing yourself, you'll never know all that's in you and what you can aim for.

There's a reason this chapter falls in the later portion of the book, rather than in the beginning. Everything you've read thus far is meant to prepare you for decisions like this. And it's worth looking at some examples of when walking away might be the best option.

Walking Away ... Into Your Future

One sign that it might be time to leave is when your psychological safety is at risk. A friend of mine once recounted a time when her manager, who was a leader at the company, told her bluntly that during her years working for the business, she had done nothing of substance and that nobody she worked with thought she did anything worthwhile. This type of speech from a leader to an employee is akin to a snake emitting poison from its fangs into a person's veins. Any outside observer would likely agree, but that doesn't make it any less difficult to decide to walk away.

My friend reflected on her manager's words and discussed with other leaders who were appalled at what had been said but didn't have the fortitude to address the issue beyond sheepishly dismissing the comments. She knew herself well enough to understand she was putting in excellent work based on her results and feedback from others, and she had the confidence to see that her work was being undervalued. It was time to move on to greener pastures and pursue a healthier route. As she explained to me, "The organization was not worth it." Leading a fulfilling life was more important to her, and when she decided to leave, she never regretted that decision. In both personal and professional relationships, if your value is constantly effaced, it can quickly become unhealthy to stick around and wait for approval.

It's worth noting that sometimes a person's value isn't judged individually, but systemically. Sadly, this is the case for some diverse employees. Several acquaintances and friends on separate occasions have shared with me that they raised concerns about discrimination related to interactions with their managers. Surprisingly, without much inquiry, their concerns were dismissed, and they were told that the managers were "great talent." It seemed the companies were more willing to bet on their instincts than understand their employees' experiences.

These accounts reflect the sad and unfortunate reality that some leaders hold an implicit bias that certain demographic groups are naturally underperforming. When organizations lead from a point of unfounded bias, they are no longer able to fulfill a fundamental commitment: serving their employees, customers, and community. Competence and capability are not confined to a specific demographic group, and yet, as a 2021 article from McKinsey & Company acknowledged, "Black employees aren't being promoted to leadership positions at the same rate as others, and this is pronounced at the most senior levels."[28] Indeed, according to McKinsey, there are four Black CEOs in Fortune 500 companies. If representation matched population demographics, there would be sixty Black CEOs. Reports about female senior leadership reveal a similar state of affairs. Currently, women account for 8.1 percent of

---

28   "Think Black CEOs Are Scarce? It's Worse Than You Think," McKinsey & Company, April 29, 2021, https://www.mckinsey.com/featured-insights/coronavirus-leading-through-the-crisis/charting-the-path-to-the-next-normal/think-black-ceos-are-scarce-its-worse-than-you-think.

CEOs at the five hundred largest American companies, based on revenue, which is the highest it has been.[29] While this indicates progress, it also serves as a sharp reminder of how far we have to go as a society. *Perhaps just as individuals need to know themselves and grow in order to give all that they can, society also needs to know itself and leverage all the tools at its disposal—including the unique value that all women and men embody—in order to become the greatest it can be.*

Notably, when my friends decided to walk away from the environments that weren't serving them, they went on to thrive and make profound impacts elsewhere. As you consider your own journey, I encourage you to always remember what is in you and what you have to offer—and strive to be in environments where the value you give is not only received but also acknowledged.

> Remember what is in you and what you have to offer—and strive to be in environments where the value you give is not only received but also acknowledged.

Walking Away ... and Getting Off Autopilot

In the stories above, my friends walked away from limiting situations to seek out environments where they could freely give all they had to offer. In my life, one person who saw my gifts and used that awareness to encourage me to walk away from comfort and toward my future was one of my first managers, a woman I was honored to work for. Her expectations were remarkably high, and she truly cared about her employees. One day, she told me, "It's apparent to me you'll need to take a different position and assume greater responsibility

---

29   Emma Hinchliffe, "The Female CEOs on This Year's Fortune 500 Just Broke Three All-Time Records," *Fortune*, June 2, 2021, https://fortune.com/2021/06/02/female-ceos-fortune-500-2021-women-ceo-list-roz-brewer-walgreens-karen-lynch-cvs-thasunda-brown-duckett-tiaa/.

soon. I'm not trying to get rid of you, but I know that by keeping you here, I'm holding you back."

I didn't want to hear the words my manager was uttering, even if I knew they were true. I was comfortable in the position I was in and was thriving in the role. My coworkers, friends, and family all recognized that I was on a great path. Yet as I reflected more, I realized that the path I was on would only lead to incremental growth. My manager was suggesting that I needed to be on a path of exponential growth.

Walking away from a bad situation might be alluring, but walking away from a good situation is not so easy. Who doesn't love the feeling of comfort? It's a wonderful feeling to understand the lay of the land at a company and how you get stuff done. And it can be terrifying to think of jumping into a new space where you have to find your bearings all over again while having to prove your worth to those around you.

And yet—isn't this what thriving is all about? If you use autopilot enough, you can forget how to drive. Staying too long in your comfort zone can dull your skills and lead you to devalue your innate abilities. Sometimes, you're not walking away from something—you're simply walking toward something else and trusting that whatever you find there will be worth it.

As Ann Landers said, "Some people believe holding on and hanging in there are signs of great strength. However, there are times when it takes much more strength to know when to let go and then to do it." Walking away is hard. But as these stories demonstrate, knowing yourself and being confident, along with your other essentials that I hope you've gained an appreciation for over the course of this book, can make the decision manageable. No matter what, remember what's in you and walk toward opportunities that will enable you to grow and to give all you can.

How to Walk Away

Over the course of my life, I noticed a unique pattern: I tended to exit situations that didn't serve me with great zeal. This was because, from a tender age, I was frequently immersed in new situations, and to cope I learned to view change as an adventure and an opportunity to explore. So I approach most change with great anticipation. However, we are all different, and when it comes to making the decision to walk away, there isn't a one-size-fits-all approach.

Each person leads a unique life based on their abilities, experiences, strengths, and shortcomings. Everyone's path is different, and it's important to make decisions that you can stand behind. Nonetheless, there are basic things we can all consider so that the decisions we make lead us down the path we aspire to.

Most fundamentally, it's important to take stock of where you stand in all aspects, including emotionally, financially, and health-wise before you walk away or walk toward something else. All change is risky to some degree, and it is important to assess the risk level you are comfortable with at a given time. It's also important to seek support from credible sources. Over the years, I've worked with both life coaches and therapists to help me unwind my past and muster the strength to pursue a direction forward that would be reflective of my values. And of course, there is an endless amount of reading you can pursue to understand what has worked or not worked for others when it comes to making changes. All of this will enable you to imagine what options could be available to you with any decisions you choose to make.

Knowing yourself and how much risk you can tolerate is a good baseline from which to start making such decisions. The following are some additional strategies that can help you reflect on the opportunities before you and help you walk away with surer footing.

Don't Ignore the Lessons

Sometimes, when we decide to walk away, it might be tempting to brand what we are leaving behind as utterly useless. But even the most painful experiences can teach us something valuable. And it is important to glean any ounce of value that we can from these situations. To do so, we must avoid simply remembering the negatives while neglecting the lessons we might take with us. Sometimes, it might take a while to realize what those lessons are. Indeed, we might have to take three, four, or five steps forward before we realize the lessons from our past that might well serve us in our future. You might not get to your desired end today or even tomorrow, but by being diligent and patient, you can begin to build a path to the future you desire.

Anchor on Where You Are Going

Sometimes when we decide to make a move, our minds are anchored on those experiences that left a sour taste in our mouth. And that can serve as the main motivation for us to leave. While this is normal, it is beneficial to get to a place where the driving motivation for walking away is where you're headed, rather than what you're leaving behind.

Knowing the personal, professional, and psychological benefits of where we are going enables us to walk away with confidence from situations that don't serve us. Perfection is an illusion. Even with the greatest hopes and promises, wherever you go will not be perfect. But heading into a situation with realistic expectations of both the challenges you might face and the benefits you might reap will help orient your mind toward reality and ultimately help you move on in a healthier way.

Walk Away—Don't Run

Your prized value is what you're able to cultivate in yourself and give to others. For example, the intelligence or knowledge that you might acquire from reading is beneficial, but using what you know to add value to others' lives is how the strength of that gift is truly displayed. In order to thrive, it's important to take the time to understand whether in your current state or environment you are truly able to give all you can, or whether the strength of your essence—what is truly great about you at the core—is slowly being depleted.

If the latter is the case, take the time to find out what changes can be made to improve the situation—a conversation with a specific individual, perhaps, or a change of responsibility. When reasonable options have been considered and you come to an understanding that true change cannot be expected or trust is broken beyond repair, then staying in your environment could be a devastating mistake.

In the last chapter, we discussed how thinking right can help us avoid regret—this message rings true here as well. Walk, don't run, from your situation. Take the time to learn from your situation so when you do leave, you can do so knowing you've truly made the right call.

Reflect and Imagine …

Taking a close look at our environments and paying attention to our reactions to them can give us important insights about whether we should stay within them or embark on something new. With that in mind, consider the following prompts in your reflection:

Does my environment inhibit me or my growth?

Are my superpowers continuously dimmed in this environment, despite my attempts to effect change?

Why am I staying in this environment? Remember that while there are many different communities in this world that we can join, it's important to find communities where we can thrive.

• • •

I believe there is a reason why each of us rises each day, and we each have something to offer. For me, time spent in an environment where I am not fulfilling my unique mission is time wasted. I am not here to simply exist—I am here to thrive, and I think you are too. In lots of situations in life, our hearts leave a lot sooner than our bodies do. When this happens, don't let yourself become like one of those wilting bouquets left on the table. Instead, I hope you'll use the lessons outlined above to walk away from what's not serving you and toward an environment where your gifts can blossom.

CHAPTER 12

Don't Shut the Door in Your Face

Sometimes things aren't clear right away. That's where you need to be patient and persevere and see where things lead.

—MARY PIERCE

As I mentioned in the last chapter, there is a common expression that states: where one door closes, another door opens. But that expression neglects to say who, exactly, is doing the closing and opening. Sometimes in life, doors close on us: we don't get the job we wanted, or our partner leaves us, or an important deal falls through, through no apparent fault of our own. Similarly, some doors seem to open of their own volition: opportunities fall in our laps without us having to do a single thing at all. However, as you begin to intentionally create the life you want to live, you'll find that it will more often than not fall to you to close the doors you need to, and open new ones. Great opportunities often lie behind doors that seem to be shut, and it's up to us to grab the knob and push it open.

Of course, that's easier said than done. After all, doors are by definition a barrier to entry. They don't just naturally swing open—they require a little effort to get through. Can you think of a time in your own life when you've stood at the threshold between the known and the unknown and neglected to push through? Perhaps you've denied yourself opportunities to add value and seek fulfillment. Or perhaps you've decided not to dream, dare, or aspire because you didn't think you were deserving or were afraid of being disappointed. Sometimes, staying where we are is just fine. Other times, we aren't just refusing to turn the doorknob—we're actually shutting the door on our own face. Failing to act out of fear or doubt can hurt us more than we know, and it's a surefire way to put an early end to a potentially thrilling journey into the unknown.

If chapter 11 was all about learning how to close the door that leads to a dead end in our lives, then chapter 12 is all about how to muster the courage to open the door to whatever exciting future awaits us. As you've read throughout part 4, what you believe drives what you do—and with that in mind, courage isn't as much of an action as it is a mindset that empowers you to stay the course on your journey and see it through to the end. If you have a mind of courage, then nothing will be able to stop you from opening whatever door awaits you and meeting whatever challenges and opportunities lie beyond the threshold.

The Courage to Stand Alone

More often than not, shutting the door in your own face translates into a kind of denial, whether it be denial of opportunities, of potential, or of possibility. And more often than not, this instinctive reaction is rooted in a deep fear. But having courage does not mean being fearless. In fact, it means practically the opposite! Courage is defined as the "mental and moral strength to venture, persevere, and withstand danger, fear, or difficulty."[30] It is the mindset that allows us to act in spite of our fears. When we do the opposite, acting *because*

---

30   "Courage," definition and meaning, Merriam-Webster, accessed November 19, 2021, https://www.merriam-webster.com/dictionary/courage.

of our fears, we remove the possibility of growth. Can you think of a time when you've shut the door too soon out of fear for what was lurking on the other side?

I once knew a woman named Jan whose job was to strengthen a senior leadership team in a large multinational company. The organization wanted to hire a director for a key position and asked five leaders to interview six candidates. All five leaders recommended the same person for the position. Since their decision was unanimous, they were convinced the candidate they selected was the final choice. To their surprise, however, their boss decided to hire an entirely different candidate without seeking their perspectives on those they interviewed. His decision bothered them, and they vented among themselves and asked Jan, "Why were we asked to spend hours assessing different candidates if our perspective wasn't even worth considering?"

Though the leaders were all troubled, none of them wanted to express their frustration to their boss, because he was known to be vindictive when given negative feedback. Since there was no easy resolution, the situation became a major distraction for their teams. As the leaders began looking to Jan for help, she was faced with a key decision: she could either speak the truth to their boss, risking annoying him and potentially putting her job at risk, or she could stay silent and lose the respect of the leaders.

As Jan reflected, she didn't agree with the way the boss handled the situation either. And amid the chaos surrounding his decision, she knew that remaining silent was a bad idea. So she decided to channel her inner superhero and share her concerns with the boss. When she did, he viewed her feedback as a direct criticism and was angered by her audacity to share it. His response worried her, and she wondered if she should've remained silent as the other leaders did. But deep down, she knew that speaking up was the right thing to do, even if she had to stand alone and the end result wasn't what she'd hoped for.

After several discussions with the boss where Jan sought to understand his perspective while upholding the validity of her opinion, they made progress toward understanding each other. As it turned out, he had not consulted with the other leaders before he made his decision because he was afraid they would contest his decision! With this understanding, Jan and the boss pulled the leaders together to have a candid conversation in which everyone had the opportunity to express themselves. This led to a number of heated discussions over some time, but it helped build trust in the organization and facilitated Jan's job in strengthening the team.

In her book *Daring Greatly*, Brené Brown writes, "Truth and courage aren't always comfortable, but they are never weaknesses."[31] In this story, both the leaders and the boss were afraid to speak up—and they and their teams suffered for it. Both parties shut the door in their own faces. But by being courageous, even though it meant standing alone, Jan demonstrated how choosing to open that door could lead to more beneficial and healthier outcomes.

How to Step Up When You're Called

Fear often arises when we realize being courageous could mean standing alone. But those moments when we choose to do what we know is right are also the times we experience the greatest fulfillment, making an impact on both our lives and the lives of others.

One of the toughest things to do is to take action in spite of fear, and fear often arises when we realize being courageous could mean standing alone. But those moments when we choose to do what we know is right are also the

---

31   Brown, *Daring Greatly*.

times we experience the greatest fulfillment, making an impact on both our lives and the lives of others. Denying ourselves the opportunity to be courageous and authentic often leads to diminishing ourselves. So how can we find the courage to rise to the occasion when we're called and give the most we can?

I once worked with a business leader, Patricia, whose opinion was requested regarding where to invest resources in the organization. Patricia's team was responsible for developing the product that generated the highest profit in the organization. One of her peers led a team that was responsible for producing a new product that was targeted at international markets. Though that product was in its nascent stage and not yet profitable, it was aimed at key international markets, which were integral to the company's strategic plan.

Understanding the strategic direction of the company and the positive impact that her peer's team could have on its long-term success, Patricia advocated for her peer's team to receive more resources than her own team. And she did so knowing her decision could result in losing the respect of her team if they felt they didn't get more resources because she "lost a battle" or, worse yet, was weak and didn't "fight" hard enough for her team.

In effect, Patricia's decision to prioritize the success of the greater organization above her individual needs could be a limiting decision, but it wasn't because of her approach. Believing her team was highly capable, she articulated the rationale for her decision to them, telling them how it would set them up for long-term success. She then solicited her team's candid perspectives and suggestions, which allowed them to share their thoughts, including the negative ones, and collectively come up with a go-forward plan. As a result, she garnered the respect of her team, her peers, and others who viewed her as a strong leader, capable of approaching problems with a strategic and balanced perspective.

Being courageous allows you to lead your life with a focus on the future instead of the past or present. It means not letting your fears hold you back from a better tomorrow. Patricia had the courage to bet on her company's future, as well as her own team's abilities. And because she worked through her fears, she helped to position her company for greater long-term success.

> Thriving personal and professional relationships are grounded in "me, you, and us," the willingness of each person to take responsibly and give sacrificially in order to create what is needed.

Patricia's decision was based on her understanding of one key principle: thriving personal and professional relationships are grounded in "me, you, and us," the willingness of each person to take responsibly and give sacrificially in order to create what is needed. In Patricia's situation, this principle translated into an understanding of the requests, contributions, and sacrifices that she needed to make to ensure her team and the organization as a whole were well positioned for the future. Below are a few pointers to help you build courage and step up to the plate when others around you need your gifts the most.

Focus On the Bigger Picture and Think in the Long Term

In Jan's story, she dared to rock the boat in the hopes of a better future. In Patricia's story, she made sacrifices in the hopes of creating a better future. Both Jan and Patricia displayed visionary courage and were willing to take the leap to make a better future their reality. When we are primarily concerned with short-term success, we aren't thriving; we are simply surviving. We aren't anticipating the needs of the future; we are merely reacting to the needs of today. Not shutting the door in your own face requires having the courageous mindset to trust that your vision for what could be is worth pursuing. Courage is the essential tool we need to bring our vision to life, no matter how long it takes.

Consider What Doors You're Shutting

In chapter 11, we discussed how to walk away—how to intentionally shut the door on circumstances that do not benefit you. It's also worth considering what doors you might be unintentionally shutting and why. How are you limiting yourself? What are you not considering? With a courageous mindset, we take risks believing the outcome would be worth it. How much risk are you willing to take on? Remember, it's impossible to live up to your full potential without taking a risk. And just because you've opened a door doesn't mean you can't close it again if you don't like what you see.

Consider What You Are Protecting

Imagine a friend hears about an opening for her dream job and applies for the job, but upon hearing that several other candidates have applied for the same position decides to withdraw her application out of fear that she might not get the job. Surely, the natural question to ask would be: Why are you holding yourself back? In many situations, we could benefit by asking the same of ourselves. What am I protecting? You see, courage enables us to have what perfection prevents us from getting. Perfection sets arbitrary limits around what we can achieve, while courage helps us figure out where those limits truly lie.

> Courage enables us to have what perfection prevents us from getting. Perfection sets arbitrary limits around what we can achieve, while courage helps us figure out where those limits truly lie.

Perfectionism is based on meeting a standard that is often set by others. Courage enables us to grow and push past preset standards. Perfectionism abhors mistakes. Courage empowers us to grow from our mistakes. Courage is not an end in itself; it is a means to an end, and that end is growth.

Arbitrarily refusing to open the door that is in front of us is often a self-protective choice. Consider what you are protecting and why. Are you willing to test the limits you've set for yourself, and expand beyond them to uncharted territory?

Reflect and Imagine …

As you approach the final part of this book, courage is the last tool you'll want to consider adding to your toolbox to strive for your dreams. Don't shut the door on your future—you never know how far you can go. Here are some ways you can put your courage to good use.

Reflect on an opportunity you are considering rejecting. Perhaps it's an opportunity to join a team, build a relationship, or engage in a developmental activity. Why do you want to say no? Is your reasoning rooted in fear or discomfort? What could you gain by saying yes? Perhaps form a lifelong friendship or build a vital skill?

Where in your life can you demonstrate courage today? Perhaps speaking up in a meeting to offer a different perspective, or initiating a relationship with someone you find impressive yet intimidating. What's a good first step? If you need help, consider asking a friend.

• • •

As Mary Anne Rademacher said, "Courage does not always roar. Sometimes courage is the quiet voice at the end of the day saying, 'I will try again tomorrow.'" Opening the door to our future takes patience and perseverance, and it takes a lot of courage. When you are ready to take action, you might be fearful. That's normal. Change is hard. Oftentimes, it's also incremental, occurring over time and not right away. Regardless of what changes you aspire to make, I hope you find the courage to turn the knob and see what's out there. In the final part of the book, that's exactly what we'll discuss: making your move. Are you ready?

PART 5

FIND YOUR ELIXIR

CHAPTER 13

Be Brave

Above all, be the heroine of your life, not the victim.

—NORA EPHRON

Hundreds of years ago, before the Scientific Revolution and the Enlightenment, cultures all over the civilized world practiced an art called alchemy. A heady mix of philosophy and natural science, alchemy was the ancient practice of transmutation: the transformation of a lesser substance into something greater—of a metal like lead, for instance, into precious gold. To perform their work, the great alchemists endlessly searched for a legendary substance said to have the power to transform whatever it touched. With its help, ill patients could become well again, and perhaps, it was believed, with the right substance, mere mortals could even conquer their own deaths to live forever.

The essence of rose is a substance that perfectly encapsulates the sweet smell of that special flower. The essence of jojoba or other flowers captures much the same. Similarly, the magical substance so sought after by practitioners of alchemy was the essence of change itself. And they called it an elixir.

Your journey through this book is now nearly complete. In these chapters, you've explored the depths of your individuality, you've reflected on the limitations of perfectionism versus the endless potential of growth, and you've considered what habits and beliefs are serving you and which are holding you back. In the last section, you've learned how to stay true to your own road map guiding you toward greatness. And in the last chapter, you've come to an understanding that courage is the mindset you'll need in order to take action. Now, armed with the growing knowledge of who you are and bolstered by the understanding that a mindset of courage can help you make the leap toward your greatest dreams, just one question remains:

Are you ready?

Are you ready to process your fears to take action? Now that you've found your path, are you ready to take it? The pages of this book were written to help you accomplish one life-altering task: create your life by using your superpowers to give what only *you* can uniquely give. Are you ready to create it?

The alchemists believed the substance of change they sought was somewhere hidden in the earth. But perhaps they were missing the point. What if the essence of change is not "out there" at all but is in fact within each of us, embedded in our very spirits? What if the elixir of transformation is not some potion but rather an emotion we can each harness? The title of this section is "Find Your Elixir." I believe that within each of the chapters contained in this book, you'll find a vital building block of that elixir of change within yourself. And it is my hope that by the time you reach the final pages of this book, you'll have found that substance within your heart and soul that encourages you to create and to live the life you've always dreamt of—not as a passive figure but as an active builder of your future.

> Create your life by using your super-powers to give what only *you* can uniquely give.

Creation starts with a knowing, and it is realized with a series of actions. In this chapter, you'll begin that exciting step forward, and it all starts with a hefty dose of bravery.

Be Brave for Yourself

At this point in your journey, you understand your worth and what you can give, and you know what's on the table. And yet, if you still felt scared when I asked if you were ready to take action, I want to remind you: You don't have to conquer every fear before you begin!

But as you read the introduction to this chapter, perhaps you were faced with another feeling: inadequacy. Many of us associate real change with epic acts of bravery—of self-sacrifice or the kind of heroism we only see in the movies. If you considered your own goals and dreams in this context and found them to be lacking, I want to gently remind you: change isn't always a monumental upheaval or a single act. And being brave is about so much more than heroic valor. Your goals don't have to be big in order for them to spark change in your life—they just have to be important and meaningful enough for you to be willing to act on them. And that's where real bravery occurs.

The Greek philosopher Heraclitus famously said, "The only constant in life is change." Indeed, changes big and small occur in our lives every single day, and sometimes they just happen to us. But what does it take to drive change rather than simply react to it? If courage is a mindset to help you move forward in spite of your fears, then bravery is an action. To be brave for yourself is to truly get comfortable with change, to find ways to thrive when it inevitably arises, and to harness the power of change to help you realize your dreams.

If change is a constant, that means the risk, uncertainty, and loss that inevitably accompany it are constants too. With every new undertaking, we often leave treasures and memories behind as we face uncertain prospects before us. Having led a life characterized by a significant amount of change, most of it involuntary in my earlier years and self-instigated in my latter years, I can certainly relate to the constancy of change and know that it can be very hard. But I have also learned that change often presents opportunities to either do something better or do something new, in a manner that benefits yourself and others. With every loss we must confront in the face of change, we are offered a chance to find something new, something special and perhaps greater than what we lost to begin with.

An Olympic hurdler understands that the obstacles in her way are mere challenges to be overcome, and as she dares to jump over them every time she practices, she gets better and better at conquering those challenges. We can view change in a similar manner—not as an obstacle but as both an inevitability and a chance to improve.

When we are brave for ourselves, daring to meet changes and obstacles head-on, we learn to live and act amid uncertainty and loss, rather than letting ourselves be conquered by our fears and doubts. In this light, any action we take toward our goals, no matter how large or small, is a brave one, because positive change is rarely a singular event but rather the product of embracing a series of opportunities. Being brave means taking action, again and again, transforming our behavior so that it aligns ever closer to our true values and our vision for the future.

> Positive change is rarely a singular event but rather the product of embracing a series of opportunities. Being brave means taking action, again and again, transforming our behavior so that it aligns ever closer to our true values and our vision for the future.

Be Brave for Others

As we've discussed in prior chapters, our values come into play most frequently in our relationships with others. After all, if your superpower is that thing that you can uniquely give, there must be a receiver on the other end to receive it! The beauty of our superpowers emerges when we are in service of others. So while being brave for ourselves is vitally important, sparking within us the will to act on our beliefs and realize our dreams, being brave for others is equally vital to our journey. Therefore, as we intentionally put our superpowers to use, being brave for both ourselves and for those in our midst go hand in hand.

I once did some consulting for a highly matrixed organization focused on redefining their strategy. The awareness of impending changes naturally gave rise to uncertainty and confusion about the future of the company among the employees. As a first step, I decided to speak with some employees. During one of these discussions, I met with a man named Chad who requested my perspective on a challenge he was experiencing.

Chad had been working in the organization for three years and had relocated across the country, leaving behind his young daughter with his mother. Chad quickly informed me that he intended to file a lawsuit on several grounds. He alleged the workplace was hostile and requested I surface his concerns with the leaders of the organization, which I did. To my surprise, some of the leaders said they'd heard Chad was also litigious with prior companies and requested I continue to discuss his concerns with him, rather than have a member of their team do so.

While throughout my career I'd worked through situations like the one Chad described, I hadn't consulted with this company for long and was concerned about the issue getting out of hand as I'd seen happen in the past. I was especially concerned as I recalled Chad's history with lawsuits. However, knowing that experience is one of the best ways to learn, I recognized that working through this issue could expedite my learning and enable me to help the organization more expeditiously.

As I listened to Chad passionately narrate his experience over the course of several discussions, I realized that while a lawsuit could be damaging to the organization, it would be devastating for him personally. As a single father raising a young daughter across the country, Chad's primary interest was his child's well-being. And engaging in a legal battle could leave him financially and emotionally drained.

I also learned that Chad was a veteran, and he viewed himself as a provider to his family and a servant to the veteran community. However, in his workplace, he felt devalued and micromanaged. He shared with me that while his leader and his teammates had a lot in common and spent time together after work, he was left out, as if he didn't "fit the mold" in spite of his skills and significant experience. The more time I spent with Chad, the more I realized the crux of his anger and decision to sue his employer were based on him feeling unheard, disrespected, and devalued. And it is amazing the extent to which a person will go in order to reclaim their power when they believe it has been usurped.

After several conversations, I relayed back to Chad what I had heard him say. I shared that I learned from our conversations how much value he was providing to his family and the veteran community. I also encouraged him to think about what mattered most to him, and then inform me of how he wanted to proceed.

A few days later, Chad called to inform me that he had given a lot of thought to our conversation and realized that his role as a father and a veteran were more important to him than engaging in a legal battle, so he had decided to leave the organization. He went on to tell me, "You've really helped me because you wanted to understand me." While Chad was grateful for what he had received from me, I felt equally grateful for the experience. It was powerful to see him grapple with anger and pain yet choose to pursue a path that was aligned to his dreams.

> When we choose to take on what scares us, in spite of the fear we feel, we can access precious gems that benefit ourselves and others.

I learned a lot from working with Chad. Most of all, I learned that when we choose to take on what scares us, in spite of the fear we feel, we can access precious gems that benefit ourselves and others.

The value I believe I can provide in this world is inextricably linked to the human beings around me. And I can find opportunities by asking people, *What matters to you? What are you working through?* We often think of bravery as loud acts of decisiveness, like a team captain's orders or the commands of an army captain in the battlefield. *But bravery can also show up in the peace and silence we provide for others—by listening, being open, and letting down our defenses rather than bolstering them further.*

I helped Chad through a difficult situation because the opportunity presented itself, and it was the right thing to do. Unexpectedly, I benefitted from it greatly. Ironically, this is what happens when we use our superpowers and are brave for others' benefit—we end up helping ourselves unintentionally in the process.

Bravery versus Bravado

Being brave can be loud or quiet. It can take place front and center or behind the scenes. Acts of bravery can change our lives or simply enable us to continue confidently on the path toward our dreams. But it's worth mentioning that, while bravery can take many forms, there's one form that it never takes: bravado. And it's important not to confuse one for the other.

While they may sound similar, bravery and bravado could not be more different. Bravery shows up as a deliberate decision driven by a strong sense of conviction to stand up, speak up, and do the right thing. Bravery is having and displaying mental, moral, and sometimes physical strength to face fear and difficulty. As Nelson Mandela said, "The brave man is not he who does not feel afraid but he who conquers that fear."[32]

Bravado, on the other hand, is a false display of "boldness," often rooted in insecurity, that is intended to influence the perception of others. Bravado is focused on what others perceive, rather than on what is real. It is grounded

---

32 "Mandela in His Own Words," CNN, accessed November 19, 2021, https://edition.cnn.com/2008/WORLD/africa/06/24/mandela.quotes/.

in an excessive need to impress. And unfortunately, these instincts can lead to pretentiousness and can stall growth, because the primary goal is not to be capable—it is simply to appear that way.

Reflect and Imagine ...

As you consider the role of bravery in your own life, remember that fears have a mystifying ability to consume us, take over our thoughts, and even drive our actions. In order to be brave, it is important to relinquish the power our fears have over us. An effective way to do so is to get close to your fear and name it. This may seem paradoxical, but by getting close to what you're afraid of, you can separate the fear from yourself. You can begin to understand that you may "feel a certain way," but not "be a certain way." For example, you may feel scared, but you are not a "coward." You may feel angry, but that doesn't mean you're an "angry person."

With this in mind, reflect on a situation that intimidates you. When you think of the situation, do you get angry or frustrated? Do you want to hide, procrastinate, or avoid the situation? Why do you feel this way? Is it because of something that happened? Or something you anticipate happening?

What can you do to diminish the power the fear has over you? Perhaps learn more about the situation?

What opportunities would be available to you if you moved forward in spite of the fear?

Who can support you as you process this situation?

• • •

Robert Louis Stevenson said, "To be what we are, and to become what we are capable of becoming, is the only end in life." Bravery is making the choice, over and over again, to live according to your most authentic values. In the next chapter, we will explore one of the greatest reasons to be brave, a reason that has the power to change not only us but the world around us: freedom.

CHAPTER 14

Chase Freedom

You can't look back; you have to keep looking forward.

—LUCY LIU

Think, for a moment, of the last time you mustered up the courage to be brave. What propelled you, in that moment, to act? Perhaps you felt compelled to act on behalf of someone who could not speak for themselves. Perhaps you were motivated by a social cause that speaks to you. Or perhaps you channeled your inner bravery to keep a promise you made to yourself in service of your own growth—maybe you challenged yourself to go out with a new friend that you find intimidating or to organize a cross-functional meeting with coworkers to brainstorm ideas. Of all the reasons you had for being brave, I bet "I had time and just wanted to see what it would be like" was not one of them.

Whether we are being brave for ourselves or for others, the actions we take are a means to an end—not an end in themselves. In other words, we are acting on purpose, for a purpose. We show bravery for a variety of reasons, such as to live our values, to grow and learn, or to demonstrate care and respect for ourselves and for others. These outcomes are what motivate us to stand up to our fears and take intentional action for a cause that matters to us.

Many of the motivations outlined above could be summed up in one word: freedom. Like bravery, this word may seem intimidatingly lofty in scope. "Freedom" conjures images of wars fought over ideals, rugged individualism, and more. But when it comes to our everyday lives, its meaning is actually quite simple and directly applicable to our lived experience. According to *The Merriam-Webster Dictionary*, freedom means "a boldness of conception or execution," "liberation," "a quality or state of being exempt or released from something onerous," and "an absence of necessity, coercion, or constraint in choice or action." At its most straightforward, freedom means "ease."

On your journey toward yourself, what are you searching for most? What is your most desired outcome? Now that you've made it this far, I'm willing to bet you're not seeking praise or fame. If I had one guess at your true purpose, I'd guess that what you're ultimately seeking here is the freedom to be yourself, to be unrestricted by the constraints of comparison, perfectionism, and other societal pressures to be, or act, or look a certain way. Freedom is the ultimate release from others' expectations of you. It is the boldness to create your own future and to make intentional choices with no strings attached. Freedom is an end in itself—a reason for acting and a reason for stepping up when you're called.

As you'll learn in this chapter, freedom is not without responsibility. It is not a pass to say whatever you want or do whatever you want at the cost of others around you. True freedom is far more nuanced than that. But when you're brave enough to chase freedom and all that it entails, you finally have all you need to write your own story. Are you ready to pick up the pen?

Chasing—and Finding—My Path to Freedom

Each and every one of us is born with a desire for freedom—to live with ease, without constraint, without hindrances, in the way we choose. And yet it seems as though, on the path toward freedom, we sometimes erect our own roadblocks. Freedom is a human right we all deserve to embrace fully. What's holding you back from embracing this right for yourself?

After living with MS for a few years, I was dismayed at the thought of what I'd lost, even though many of the losses were anticipated, not actualized. With dreadful anticipation, I feared what more I would lose as the condition progressed. I was especially afraid of falling, which would fore-shadow the loss of mobility, and so I decided to spend much of my time indoors, convinc-ing myself that even though my flat sometimes felt like a cage, I wasn't missing all that much. After all, I thought, restricting my focus to home and work allowed me to produce more professionally.

> Life is filled with both positive and negative circumstances. You create your life based on how you choose to navigate those circumstances. It always starts with a choice.

However, this wasn't the life I truly desired, and I knew it. The superheroine in me wanted to explore and enjoy all aspects of my life in spite of any challenges—but I wasn't sure how to conjure the bravery I needed to manifest the freedom I knew deep down that I wanted.

As I reflected on my personal and professional life, it occurred to me that life was happening to me, and I was just going with the flow. So I began to ponder a series of questions: Is this the life I want to live? I am successful, but am I thriving? I am breathing, but am I living? Who is creating my life? This exploration led me to an obvious but enlightening realization: life is filled with both positive and negative circumstances. You create your life based on how you choose to navigate those circumstances. It always starts with a choice.

This epiphany led me to probe how and where I spent my time. My first realization was that work was the only reason why I lived in Seattle. My loved ones were miles away on the East Coast, and suddenly, a job didn't seem like a good enough reason to be separate from them. I needed balance, and that required me to start paying attention to all facets of my life—physical, emotional, spiritual, and social—not just work. I also needed access to great healthcare and quickly learned that several renowned medical facilities with MS centers were located on the East Coast, near my family. Suddenly, moving to the East Coast felt like a clear next step.

With all the stars aligning, I decided to leave Seattle and embark on a journey to reawaken my dreams and create my life. And while I couldn't predict how my journey would unfold, I knew I was not alone. I knew who I was, and I had my faith and my team of trusted friends. Ralph Ellison said, "When I discover who I am, I'll be free." And I was finally ready to chase that freedom.

The move was scary—it always is when we walk away—and yet it was also thrilling, because I knew what I was seeking and the dreams I was pursuing. When my desires for great healthcare, being close to loved ones, and doing what I loved were finally brought together, I noticed that my physical body, heart, and mind began working as a team to create the sense of balance I longed for. This didn't mean things were perfect. But it did mean I was free. *You see, chasing freedom can be frightening, but freedom is always liberating, and it is a worthy pursuit.*

Chasing Freedom and Embracing Responsibility

Freedom is an innate human desire and a right of each and every one of us. And yet, freedom that comes at the expense of others is not freedom at all but recklessness. When freedom is exercised responsibly, others are also uplifted. It's important to exercise our freedom in a manner that does not cause undue suffering to another. While this may seem like a fine line to walk, I can think of two examples in history where individuals have demonstrated how to do so, with bravery and respect for others motivating their every step. First, I'll share their stories, then I'll outline what their stories can tell us about how to balance freedom and responsibility in our own lives.

The first person is Nelson Mandela. This universally acclaimed leader epitomized what it means to chase freedom without neglecting the responsibility that comes with it. Mandela is acknowledged globally as a leader who stood up for the rights of others by leading the resistance to apartheid in South Africa and who ultimately helped to end that brutal institution. While he eventually claimed victory over apartheid, it came at a personal cost: his efforts caused him to spend twenty-seven years behind bars. Those years could've destroyed whatever will he had left to fight. And yet, Mandela once described those years in prison as "a long holiday."[33] Referring to such a dreadful experience in such a noble manner reveals just how much Mandela was grounded in his mission to pursue freedom, no matter the obstacle. And eventually, when he was free, he persisted in his pursuit for freedom for all with grace and strength. Most of us will never have to endure that level of suffering as we pursue our dreams, but there's much to learn from his example. In his life and actions, Mandela demonstrated the true power of persistence against all odds.

The second person is Robin Cavendish. Born in 1930, Cavendish received a diagnosis of polio at the young age of twenty-eight. Paralyzed from the neck down, he was given just months to live, but somehow, he defeated those bleak odds to live for nearly four more decades, passing away at age sixty-four. When he was diagnosed, Cavendish's doctors wished to keep him in the hospital primarily because he required a medical respirator to breathe, and without that connection, he could've died at any moment. However, after a year in the hospital, he made the controversial choice to leave and live his life on his own terms by returning to his home. By leaving the hospital, he not only chased freedom for himself, but he pursued it for his family and all others in his situation. He was determined that polio survivors should have

---

33   Mike Wooldridge, "Mandela Death: How He Survived 27 Years in Prison," BBC News, December 11, 2013, https://www.bbc.com/news/world-africa-23618727.

the opportunity to heal in environments that allowed them to thrive, and he worked his entire life to see his vision through. He became one of Great Britain's strongest advocates for the disabled, founding charities and helping to create resources to make life easier for those with polio. By chasing freedom, Cavendish paved the way for others like him to chase it too.

Nelson Mandela and Robin Cavendish both pursued freedom at all costs, except for one: these men never pursued freedom at the cost of other people's well-being. What can we learn from their lives, so that we can do the same in ours? We can start by keeping in mind two important lessons, outlined below.

View Freedom as an Infinite Resource

One of the greatest fallacies about freedom is that it is a limited resource—that when one group of people has it, another group of people must lose it. In reality, freedom is not a zero-sum game. When freedom is granted to one person, it does not mean anyone needs to pay or be punished. Such a worldview is selfish, but Mandela and Cavendish both demonstrate the power of selflessness in pursuing freedom for all, rather than a select few. When Mandela became president of South Africa, he could've punished his tormenters. Likewise, when Cavendish left the hospital, he could've used his newfound freedom to only benefit himself rather than the rest of the disabled community. Instead, they viewed their freedom as an infinite resource from which everyone in their midst could benefit.

Respect the Freedom of Others

Often, when someone uses their freedom to limit others, it is out of fear that others would misuse theirs if they had the opportunity. But recognizing that others have the right to think, act, and make decisions just like you will enable you to seek to influence, rather than to subjugate. When Mandela was released from prison, he worked to put in place institutions to ensure everyone had equal access to freedom. And when he served as president of South Africa, he undoubtedly knew that in many other African countries, leaders did not respect laws concerning term limits. However, Mandela did not follow suit. Instead, he respected the term mandates, thereby modeling his intention of freedom for everyone.

Mandela's intention was to help free people, and he acted on his intention without fear while always recognizing others around him had freedoms too. As you pursue your path to freedom, I hope you remember the fearlessness that Mandela embodied and remember that others, even those with different perspectives, need not be adversaries on your path—some of them can be your allies.

> Recognizing that others have the right to think, act, and make decisions just like you will enable you to seek to influence, rather than to subjugate.

Reflect and Imagine ...

As you progress on your journey, it is important to not only focus on what you are pursuing and why, but also focus on the impact it will have on others. Specifically, as you pursue freedom, it is helpful to know what you stand to gain and what it will take to achieve your dreams. Here's a way to gain the clarity you need to chase what you desire:

Chase your dream. What's your dream? Why does it matter?

What do you need to pursue the dream? Perhaps a friend could support you.

Do you fear you do not have what it takes to realize your dream? What could that fear be holding you back from?

What will you gain if you go for your dream? Who else can you help by aiming high?

• • •

Nelson Mandela said, "To be free is not merely to cast off one's chains but to live in a way that respects and enhances the freedom of others." As you pursue a future unbridled by others' expectations or assumptions, keep in mind that all those around you are filled with the same desire for freedom as you are. Use your superpowers to find your freedom and to help others find theirs. This is one of the greatest ways we can add value. I hope you'll remember this as you proceed on your journey.

CHAPTER 15

Dare to Venture

Don't downgrade your dream just to fit your reality.
Upgrade your conviction to match your destiny.

—UNKNOWN

Dear reader, you've made it! Over the last fourteen chapters, I've pointed out some of the greatest hurdles life puts in the way of our journeys, and I've asked you to consider how you might clear them in order to become your best and truest self. Together, we've investigated what it means to truly know ourselves, how to conquer the need to be perfect, how to find confidence, when to walk away, and much more in between. Through each of these explorations, I hope you've learned lessons that you can take with you for the rest of your life.

Importantly, I believe that in knowing yourself a little bit better, you realize that when it comes to creating our lives, there is no perfect time or way to do so. And I hope you've learned to anchor yourself and your actions in authenticity so that when times get tough, you can reflect, remember, and give yourself and your future a chance.

My greatest hope of all is that somewhere in these pages, you've found the elixir of change in your heart and soul. Perhaps, little by little, step by step, you've even started to reap the rewards of viewing yourself and your circumstances in a different light.

Allan Rufus said, "Unless we take that first step into the unknown, we will never know our own potential."[34] In this final chapter, I have but one aim: to show you what amazing things can come when you dare to venture into the unknown and see what awaits you on the other side. What is available to you in your life is greater than you know. You've embarked on a great adventure to find out, and the great adventure is just beginning.

> What is available to you in your life is greater than you know.

Daring to Dream Big

Do you remember the vivid dreams you had as a child, or the sense of wonder that stirred in your heart in the middle of the night? Or the profound sense of hope and excitement you felt when you saw something that piqued your interest? Do you remember what you did with those dreams? As you got older, did you shove them away, believing they were unrealistic, or did you hang on to them, believing that someday they could materialize? Dreaming is powerful, whether we are awake or asleep. And despite what our younger selves may have believed or didn't believe, those seemingly "unattainable" dreams planted in our subconscious mind *can* be realized—it takes desire, courage, and effort.

Someone whose life has shown me what it means to dare to realize a dream is my father. My father was born in a small town in a country on the west coast of Africa called Cameroon. His father was a farmer, and his mother was a trader. As was often the case on the continent in the 1940s, sons followed in their father's footsteps. So as a young boy, my father accompanied his dad

---

34 Allan Rufus, *The Master's Sacred Knowledge: A Key to Your Inner Treasure* (CreateSpace Independent Publishing Platform, 2012).

to his farms after school, on weekends, and on vacations to work. On their farms, they grew cash crops, including cocoa and coffee for export. For daily consumption and local markets, they grew food crops, including plantains, beans, and yams. Also, my dad and his father often caught fish and prawns at a river that traversed one of their farms.

One day, when my dad was eleven years old and at their farm, he saw a group of men talking to other farmers. My dad had never seen those men before, so he was curious. He learned they were from a large organization and came to teach farmers how to get a better harvest. My dad was intrigued, and in that moment, a seed was planted in his heart. Knowing the immense value that farming and fishing provided to the community, he was inspired and decided that when he grew up, he, too, would help the community as those men were.

My father's desire to help the community was further strengthened when, at the age of thirteen, his father unexpectedly passed away. My father missed his dad deeply and hung on to the memories they shared—especially his dad's desire for him to excel and take care of his community. This, too, served as inspiration for my father to pursue his dreams and persist during tough times.

Over time, the seed planted in his heart began to take root, leading him on a worldwide adventure he could've never imagined. Being very inquisitive, my dad viewed learning as a ticket to thriving and seized the opportunity to travel across the world to attend the University of Washington, where he got a PhD in Fisheries Biology. His reason for choosing to go to the University of Washington was simple: at that time, it was the top institution for what he wanted to learn.

The men my father saw helping farmers when he was an eleven-year-old were from the Food and Agriculture Organization (FAO), a specialized agency of the United Nations that leads international efforts to defeat hunger. Through persistence and growth, my father realized his childhood dream: he worked for FAO where he led and drove responsible and sustainable fisheries policies on a global scale until he retired. Indeed, he lived out his dream to help his community and communities all over the world.

When I was younger, I asked my dad how he went from a small town in a small country in Africa to promoting a worthy cause in a global organization, all based on a childhood dream. He told me that he didn't do it alone. Through every obstacle, he remembered his dad's work ethic and the value to the community the men he saw helping farmers had provided. He also knew he had an unshakeable partnership with my mother, whom he fondly refers to as his "April bride of over half a century," and the devotion of several friends to help him along his journey. All of this enabled him to remain optimistic and pursue his dream, despite its seemingly unattainable nature.

> We all have dreams, even if we have forgotten them, and each of us has superpowers, even if we don't know what they are right away. Through the course of our lives, every single day, we have the power to write our own story.

As Simon Sinek says, "Optimism is not the denial of difficult times. Optimism is the belief that the future is bright."[35] Thinking about our own futures this way benefits us greatly, because it reminds us to not be deterred by what we think is impossible, but instead to remember that through adversity, we can grow and give what only we can uniquely give.

We all have dreams, even if we have forgotten them, and each of us has superpowers, even if we don't know what they are right away. Through the course of our lives, every single day, we have the power to write our own story.

---

35 Simon Sinek, "Optimism vs. Positivity," YouTube, April 6, 2020, https://www.youtube.com/watch?v=roDLXM70du0.

Can you imagine how different the world would be if each of us had the courage to do so, instead of letting others write it for us?

• • •

Remember, the world needs you and your uniqueness. It needs your strength, and it needs your vulnerability. It needs your kindness and your confidence. And others in your circle need you too. The possibility of realizing one's dreams and contributing to the well-being of others was an inspiration for this book. I hope it continues to inspire you, over and over, as you live life to its fullest.

Conclusion

You are braver than you believe, stronger than you seem, and smarter than you think.

—A. A. MILNE, *WINNIE THE POOH*

As you reflect on the ideas this book has presented to you and venture out, who is standing beside you? Chasing freedom and finding our very own elixir for change is not a one-person job. When you envision your future, who are you fighting for? And who is fighting for you?

This journey is about you, and it's about your people—the people who support you, and who you want to support. You see, this is how the world changes. With one small act at a time. With one individual, using her superpowers to do good, not with brute strength but with kindness, intentionality, and bravery and with the clear knowledge that when she falls, she can get up again.

Through the course of our lives, we face situations that make us doubt ourselves and question our abilities. In those moments, each of us has to wrestle with key questions: How will I respond to these challenges? Will I let them consume me and render me powerless, or will I view them as opportunities to learn, grow, and give what only I uniquely can? These are also opportune moments to step out in courage and pursue the truth, armed with the knowledge of who you are and the support of your trusted friends. Through adversity, you can lead a life where your body, heart, and mind work in unison to propel you forward. What is required to do so is no small task—but it is a worthwhile task.

While there is no known cure for MS today, I hope and confidently believe there will be one in the future. I also hope and believe there will be remedies for many other illnesses that plague society. For me, I still take infusion treatments for MS, and I still get MRI scans that show signs of irregularity, the effects of which I feel every day. And, like all of us, I have moments when I'm frustrated and wonder why I have to deal with life's challenges. But soon after each of those moments, I remember that my superheroine abilities can enable me to thrive and create a life that is worth living. And I know the importance of thinking right.

You see, one of the most pivotal lessons I've learned through physical therapy is that what we are able to do often starts with how we think. When we think right, we can summon the courage and take brave actions that enable us to pursue our dreams. As I continue on my journey, I also know what it takes to find balance. And most importantly, I know that I am not alone in this journey of life, that I have an Overarching Force and forces accompanying me and propelling me along the right pathways. It was never intended for any of us to become perfect or to navigate life alone. The greater aspiration is to truly live and seek fulfillment, to grow and to help others.

Thank you for letting me be a part of your magnificent journey to and through self-knowledge and understanding. I hope you take a chance on yourself and dare to venture.

DARE TO VENTURE

My past cannot predict my future

I've come too far to let my destiny rupture

Pain is a memory to which I bear no allegiance

My hallmark has been persistence

Fiercely seeking the indescribable

Could my vision be attainable?

Through silvery shadows, a thought arises

To the depths of my soul, it nudges

My course shall be marked by endurance

The adversity I have faced will lead to balance

Let forgotten dreams be remembered

Let muted words be uttered

My greatest loss would be to deprive the world of what's in me

Fulfillment awaits me

I will dare to venture.

—AKÉ SATIA

Some Gems

Throughout my life, I have been fortunate to stand on the shoulders of many giants. As you continue on your journey, I would like to share some great pieces of work that have empowered me. With gratitude to all who have shared deliberately.

- *The Gifts of Imperfection*, Brené Brown
- *Nonviolent Communication: A Language of Life*, Marshall B. Rosenberg
- *Becoming*, Michelle Obama
- *Start with Why*, Simon Sinek
- *Man's Search for Meaning*, Viktor Frankl

Resources

Multiple Sclerosis Foundation: https://msfocus.org/
Multiple Sclerosis Society of America: https://mymsaa.org
Pulmonary Embolisms: Mayo Clinic

About the Author

A citizen of the world, Aké Satia grew up across three continents: Africa, Europe, and North America. In her professional career, she spent almost two decades working for large global corporations, helping organizations thrive by seizing opportunities to grow, develop, and harness the unique qualities of their people. She currently consults with organizations across different industries and of varying sizes. Some of her focus areas include helping organizations identify their strategic value and transform, as well as strengthen their workforce, crush their goals, and create their desired future.

Aké believes the best way to gain knowledge is to explore, and to learn from and with others. She has a keen appreciation for reading and for exploring different cultures and is a lifelong enthusiast of the arts, especially literature and visual arts.

Aké cares deeply about children and believes we can create a world where future generations can flourish. She enjoys long, unstructured conversations with friends; dark chocolate; and being near, on, and in the water. She belongs to a very close family and enjoys being a daughter, sister, aunt, and friend.

Aké is currently based in the Free State of Maryland.

www.akesatia.com
Don't just imagine your future. Create it.

Printed in the USA
CPSIA information can be obtained
at www.ICGtesting.com
JSHW011554190224
57673JS00019B/710